PRAISE FOR THE SECOND EDITION

In this revised and expanded second edition of a book that she published in 2016 while a second-year doctoral student, Dr. Ayo Sekai uses poetry to reimagine academic scholarship, assert her voice as a linguistic scholar, and reclaim the narrative of her identity and heritage as an Afro-descendant. In doing so, she skillfully positions poetic activism as a potent nexus of art, literature, storytelling, and philosophical expression of societal worldview. This book offers a stimulating and innovative approach to the intellectual renewal and celebration of transcendental Africanity.

—Mohamed S. Camara, PhD
Professor and Chair, Department of African Studies
Editor-in-Chief, *Howard Journal of African Studies*
Howard University

From the forceful poetic contents embedded in the second edition of A^2, Dr. Molefi Kete Asante says of Dr. Ayo Sekai, "[She] is the newest generation in a long line of royal panoply, including Haki Madhubuti, Nikki Giovanni, Mari Evans, Sonia Sanchez, and Langston Hughes." A product of Howard University's graduate program and its Political Science Department, Dr. Sekai pulls from both her acquired academic knowledge and her lived experiences to provide a unique volume of Afrocentric thought and presents a voice that reflects the struggles and concerns throughout the diaspora. She does this while weaving reflective poetry through her content. Dr. Sekai uniquely uses poetry as the political framework of her volume. It is clearly worth reading.

—Henry T. Frierson, PhD
Professor Emeritus
Past Associate Vice President and Graduate School Dean
College of Education
University of Florida

At 16 years old, Dr. Ayo Sekai penned the poem "South Africa," poignantly weaving political activism, African consciousness, and the spirit of the ancestors. Her passion for Black people was so evident and powerful that I included it on my CD track "Short Takes," released in 1992. As a self-trained musician, a bassist who began playing music at 12 years old, I recognized in Dr. Sekai the same defiance that moves me in my music and propels me to play the sounds of the *Souls of Black Folk* (W. E. B. Du Bois). Watching her evolve into the force of nature she is now is the manifestation of the hope of the slave, passing the torch of liberation and combining the synergies of words, like music notes writing the revolution in scholarship.

—Lonnie Plaxico
Bassist, Composer, Producer
Double Bass and Bass Guitar
Louis Armstrong Jazz Award
LonniePlaxico.com

As a social science press, UWP stretches the boundaries of inclusion beyond the norms of Eurocentric frameworks, exemplified in Dr. Ayo Sekai's cutting-edge approach to research, implementing an innovative methodology to examine and present findings. A^2 is a masterfully woven, soul-filling prose substantiated with academic documentation elevating the messages as sage counsel and legendary storytelling contextualizing our experiences. Legitimizing the lived experiences of the African diaspora, she treats us with her linguistic expertise digging through the catacombs of history, reigniting as witness, with a call to activism.

—Ann-Marie Waterman, PhD
Chief of Staff, Coppin State University
Author, "Privatizing Education" in *Newschaser: The Rhetoric of Trump in Essays and Commentaries* (Harris, 2017)

The Sankofa symbol is believed to represent a duality in life, honoring the past while moving toward the future. Dr. Ayo Sekai's scholarly contribution of multidisciplinary dichotomy presents readers, as well as the academy, with a new direction in scholarship and academic research. This framework elevates and combines the traditional approach of a singular direction with the power of lyricism and the spoken word to infuse the research phenomenon with an intricate complexity. With the traditions of scholastic research in a powerful union unlocking the doors of creativity and scholarship to promote new ideas and new avenues for study, Dr. Sekai's current work is expanding the research trajectory in a cohesive manner, enhancing the canon of research with inclusion of ideas as opposed to exclusion. The approach from Dr. Sekai is revolutionary in design yet includes all the integrity of the high standards of rigorous academic scholarship.

—Lester J. Bentley, PhD
Clinician, African American Child Wellness Institute
Professor, Augsburg University

PRAISE FOR THE FIRST EDITION

Dr. Ayo Sekai grapples with the most important questions of our time. Reflecting on her own evolving identity within the complex racial and ethnic reality of today's America, she elucidates universal truths about the human experience. Using poetry, she will enlighten every reader, scholar, and thought leader in innumerable ways.

—Rachel May, PhD
Associate Professor
Director, Institute for the Study of Latin America
and the Caribbean (ISLAC)
University of South Florida (USF)
Author, *Terror in the Countryside: Campesino Responses to Political Violence in Guatemala, 1954–1985*

The great Civil War "general" Harriet Tubman both loved and forcefully persuaded her enslaved charges onward to freedom—some against their will and others who had faith that the uncomfortable journey would end in triumphant reward. Dr. Ayo Sekai's *Afrocentric Before Afrocentricity* prods scholars to shape research through self- and collective discovery, framing the nuances of language that interrogate humanity through prose as a social science against the historical, social, and political settings of the past and present. While it is an artful reflection of the strength of a people, it is also an ode to all who can appreciate the challenges and rewards of a journey toward collective liberation and intellectual freedom.

—Gwendolyn S. Bethea, PhD
Director, Speakers Bureau
Director, Preparing Future Faculty (PFF) Program
Howard University

A^2
Second Edition

To SKU

and

The Resilience of the Human Spirit

A²
A Scholarly Poetical Science Discourse
Second Edition

Ayo Sekai, PhD

Copyright © 2024 Universal Write Publications, LLC

All rights reserved. Except as permitted by U.S. copyright law, no part of this work may be reproduced or distributed in any form or by any means, or stored in a database or retrieval system, or otherwise, without written permission from the publisher, except in the case of newspapers, magazines, and websites using quotations embodied in critical essays and reviews.

All third-party trademarks referenced or depicted herein are included solely for the purpose of illustration and are the property of their respective owners. Reference to these trademarks in no way indicates any relationship with, or endorsement by, the trademark owner.

Printed in the United States of America

23 24 25 26 27 10 9 8 7 6 5 4 3 2 1

Mailing/Submissions:
Universal Write Publications, LLC
421 8th Avenue, Suite 86
New York, NY 10116

Website: UWPBooks.com

ISBN: 978-0-9742269-3-4

Library of Congress Control Number: 2024902725

Front Cover Designer: Cheyanne Rosier

This book has been partially supported with a financial grant from Sage Publishing.

Contents

Foreword — xi
Preface — xv
Acknowledgments — xvii

Introduction — 1

Part I. Poems With Scholarly Discourse — 15

Chapter 1. All About the Hair — 17

Chapter 2. All Woman — 25

Chapter 3. American Dream — 31

Chapter 4. The Broken Bridge — 37

Chapter 5. Compelled to Be Silent — 43

Chapter 6. Counternarrative — 47

Chapter 7. Courting Through the Drums — 53

Chapter 8. Don't Hate Me — 57

Chapter 9. The Evolution of My Child — 61

Chapter 10. Follicle Affair — 65

Chapter 11. Get Out of My Way — 71

Chapter 12. Halloween — 75

Chapter 13. Her Name Is — 85

Chapter 14. It's Been a Long Long Time — 93

Chapter 15. It's the Same Thing	103
Chapter 16. My Nubian Sisters	111
Chapter 17. Named	117
Chapter 18. Namesake Alone	123
Chapter 19. Oblivion	131
Chapter 20. A People Dying	135
Chapter 21. Pride and Prejudice	139
Chapter 22. Queen	145
Chapter 23. South Africa	151
Chapter 24. Spiritually Grounded	155
Chapter 25. A Tribute	159

Part II. Poetical Science Discourse Analysis — 163

Chapter 26. Nea Onnim	165
Poetical Analysis: African King	170
Poetical Analysis: Any Day Now	174
Poetical Analysis: Browning	178
Poetical Analysis: Coffee	182
Poetical Analysis: Disclosure	186
Poetical Analysis: The Homeless Cry	190
Poetical Analysis: I Found Me	192
Poetical Analysis: I Looked Into the Mountains	196
Poetical Analysis: Loving the Metaphor of Life	198
Poetical Analysis: Man and Child	200
Poetical Analysis: Oppression or Equal Rights	204
Poetical Analysis: Revolution	206
Poetical Analysis: Youth Crime! No More!	210

Afterword	213
Index	215
About the Author	219

Foreword

Molefi Kete Asante, PhD

"I am in awe" may be the anthem of this profoundly important book, A^2, because it has established itself in the midst of our ordinary lives. Dr. Ayo Sekai opens our eyes and our spirits with cutting-edge ideas, metaphors, tropes, and modern proverbs. Reading this book, one immediately senses the brilliance of the author who has taken on the role of bard of the times. How has she done this? She has reached into our history, aspirations, and desires and given us a book that shines because of its shiny Blackness in terms of wisdom, majesty, and monumentality.

Dr. Sekai's A^2 takes on all the barriers, obstacles, and self-doubts and with a keen eye demonstrates that the beauty of our language, dance, art, and spirit resonates with our desire to be free. African people in the United States have always sought to be liberated from the rhetoric of inferiority, discrimination, and the burden of cultural assaults. Dr. Sekai shows us through the strength of this very Afrocentric book that we have some control in our own hands. We are in the orbit of the universe, and Dr. Sekai reminds us of this in every case.

This narrative she weaves of a woman who started to see the larger horizons with the South African struggle against apartheid runs its way to a real quest for endarkenment, placing this work not just as poetry or political science but also in the discipline of history. These rumblings are a deep cry that causes her to say:

> My Nubian sisters
> It is in our hands to take hold of our future
> To rescue our men and our brothers (p. 111)

What Dr. Sekai shows us is that African Americans, Caribbean Americans, and all manner of those from the diasporas come from a long history of poets and griots with messages of lamentation and liberation that live in our collective memory. She is the newest generation in a long line of royal panoply, including Haki Madhubuti, Nikki Giovanni, Mari Evans, Sonia

Sanchez, and Langston Hughes. Now we will add the name Ayo Sekai to this list with the note that, upon publication of the first edition, she became the first poet to have the name *Afrocentric* in the title of her book. We visit and revisit the corridors of our ancestors' experiences and see ourselves reflected in the plaintive voice of the political scientist, scholar activist, and poet who seeks to know why things are the way they are at the moment. Dr. Sekai's words are painted in our minds like the brightness of Basquiat's colors.

This is a personal journey of words that is a reflection of us all. Dr. Sekai travels through the lanes of our existence by showing us where she has stood over the past years—unshaken, unwavering—and where she stands today. In this way, the work is evolutionary, moving, fluid, and meant to let us in so that we too can feel the pain and joy expertly woven into words, emotions, thoughts, and remembrance. Yet she is bold and courageous, and her poetry reaches for the heights of joyful expressions.

> The sweet smell of want and hunger would burn our souls as gift-wrapped clothes and what-nots would come spilling out of a suitcase as sweet as perfume (p. 31)

As much as the poet carries us with her into the intricate avenues of her experiences, there are places—her places—where we are still in awe of the power and the glory of the African woman. It is the hair thing that grabs us at times because it is their hair that has aggravated and caused so many women to doubt themselves, to know themselves, and to ascend to their highest moments. Hair may very well be tracked along this journey as a woman—any woman, this woman poet—moves between the unknown questioning to the definite knowledge of being herself in all her forms and ways. At one point, Dr. Sekai reveals the struggle to deal with hair in the corporate world:

> I need to have my hair done bad...
> My kinky, thick hair just don't cut it in the corporate world...
> Just need some gel
> Weave cascading down my back
> Or some sewn-in curl (p. 18)

But Dr. Sekai knows that this is just a phase of our lives that comes from the craziness of our being in an insane place in the American nation. We are who we are because we have gone through certain experiences. Our hair, as she knows, is good because it is healthy and it is ours. Whether one speaks of it or not—whether a woman wears her character, her beauty, or her crown like long coils of Black life or bound tight to the head like a cap or not the truth—is the same.

Thus, one knows in these poems that they are deeper than any physical attribute because they are made to reflect the evolution of a woman who knows something is not right with the way things are and who strives to reach the goals of inner peace. She sees in her own story and that of her people the difficult journey to sanity, and that is why she cries:

> Our people border on the line of insanity
> The journey hard and the road long
> Whips and lashes still create psychological stripes on our backs
> But we are destined to survive
> Liberating our minds is the key
> We must reach back for the hands of those who remember
> Those who look like you and me (p. 97)

Here the poet asks for a collective solution to our survival in a world that has brought us to the brink of insanity. I like the fact that she believes and tells us so expertly that we are destined to survive.

What Dr. Sekai shows us in these richly personal poems is that her journey was as long, intense, and purposeful as ours is and shall be. It carries us across many rivers and valleys of life to the realization and transformation that has made her the voice that was trying to be heard just before the burst of the Afrocentric. This is the victory.

—**Molefi Kete Asante, PhD**
Most Published African American Scholar (100 Books)
Father of Afrocentricity
Author, *Being Human Being* (2021);
Revolutionary Pedagogy (2nd ed., 2023)
Department of Africology
Temple University

Preface

Daryl Taiwo Harris, PhD

Dr. Ayo Sekai's A^2 takes us on an emancipatory journey of memory, struggle, and transformation, and speaks powerfully of Dr. Sekai's own Afrocentric trek of recovery and enlightenment. But like the indomitable Harriet Tubman, Dr. Sekai is not satisfied with her own healing and regaining of consciousness. Bound to the exigencies of Blackness, Dr. Sekai resolves to expend her considerable lyrical talent on the renewal and uplift of tens of millions of Black people; each offering in A^2, such as "Browning" (p. 178), sanctifies Black experience in all its grief, hopefulness, and delight.

As a revolutionary, she uses the power of words; as a linguistic scholar, she transforms poetry into the fluidity of social movements so academic scholarship can be transformed. Truly, the poetic device proves useful for Dr. Sekai's purposes (as is generally the case for all Black poets). She employs it to hone a message or critique a problem, ones that are externally imposed as well as those that are self-perpetuating. Black people revere the Black poet when she exhibits truth, courage, and service. And because Dr. Sekai's journey is emancipatory, we are right to anticipate that she would suggest a way forward, a way out of the European-induced malaise. It all begins, Dr. Sekai suggests, with Black love and Black acceptance of our Black selves. This helps explain why Dr. Sekai readily addresses the matter of Black beauty—hair, the skin's hue, and more. She knows these concerns very well. They are the bane of all Black women who live in anti-Black societal contexts. But in A^2, Dr. Sekai stands up and speaks out, exuding truth, courage, and service for African people and especially for African women.

Finally, Dr. Sekai's A^2 indicates very importantly that there is a process of learning or "endarkening" before Afrocentricity can be claimed or realized, which is to stand and act on one's own historical and cultural terms. Her strong belief in character, and the core of her endeavors, is passion, not for herself but for those who look like her, and the deep desire to bring along those who care enough to walk alongside her in the liberation of fairness and justice. In her work, her ache is palpable, her yearning for racial equity intense. This book is a journey into oneself, to reflect. It is not an attempt to point fingers or bring more divisiveness. It is instead an interrogation of what we already know, and an invitation for collaboration to find our way out.

—**Daryl Taiwo Harris, PhD**
Author, *Newschaser* (2017)
Chair, Political Science Department
Howard University

Acknowledgements

I *am* because of My Village, My Faith, My Foundation.

With immense gratitude to the readers, students, professors, fellow scholars, booksellers, supporters, and critics; for choosing to spend your time in my words and finding me worthy of your encouragement or advice and opportunities for growth.

To my mentor, Dr. Molefi Kete Asante, who supports me and encourages me to move forward and take the steps necessary for the manifestation of my scholarly endeavors. To my mentor and academic advisor, Dr. Daryl Taiwo Harris, chair of Howard University's Political Science Department, who continues to nurture, support, and guide me. To Geane deLima, the tiny giant, with a big heart and mighty roar, and my conspiratress. Forever the *Director* (you and I know).

In every way I show up, my character, my heart on my sleeves, my intense capacity to love, and my deep gratitude are made manifest through the three great loves of my life: Isaac, my *rock*; Cheyanne Alexandra; and Alexander Isaac. You are my inspiration, my muse, my caretakers, and my advisors. Everything I am is because of you. To my family (of blood, by choice, through adoption, or claimed by the spirit), I love you all, and I couldn't possibly repay you for your wisdom, for your friendship, for telling me the truth, and for tilting my head up when it bows. It is because of you that I continue to grow. It is because of you that I continue to thrive. It is because of you that I can give so deeply to the world, knowing there is no gratitude at the end of the rainbow, just the knowledge that I have lived my truth, and that is enough.

To my editors, book designer, proofreaders, and conspirators: *Thank you!*

Introduction

> Yes, the first duty of the colonized poet is to clearly define the people, the subject of his creation. We cannot go resolutely forward unless we first realize our alienation. We have taken everything from the other side. Yet the other side has given us nothing except to sway us in its direction through a thousand twists, except lure us, seduce us, and imprison us by ten thousand devices, by a hundred thousand tricks. To take also means on several levels being taken. It is not enough to try and disengage ourselves by accumulating proclamations and denials. It is not enough to reunite with the people in a past where they no longer exist. We must rather reunite with them in their recent counter move which will suddenly call everything into question: we must focus on that zone of hidden fluctuation where the people can be found, for let there be no mistake, it is here that their souls are crystallized and their perceptions and respiration transfigured.
>
> —Frantz Fenon, *The Wretched of the Earth* (2004, p. 163)

The poems in this book represent a colonized people. And I am a colonized poet. These methods of poetry—stanza, rhyme, assimilation, alliteration, metaphor, and others—are interwoven into the spirit of the activist, born in Jamaica, who migrated to the United States as a teenager to emerge as a woman in Brooklyn, New York, one of the boroughs where the Caribbean heart and soul beats, where language manifests as celebration, resistance, love, and revolt.

The journey in creating this book, from when it was first done to now, depicts my development as I continue to grow and immerse myself in the research of humanity. Every piece was created because I was moved to stand in the balance for a voice who was silenced, for injustice where I felt helpless, for emotions that make us human, and for experiences that make this life worth living. This book was never about poetry; it is and will always be about the power of words, a fight against linguicide in all its forms of expression. These pieces of creative work are instruments for understanding and reconciling language in space, and how human beings are impacted through the construction of race, the politics that police it, and behaviors that reinforce its structure and construction. My linguistic scholarship touches on glottopolitics and raciolinguistics in their relationship to the movement of Black people, linguicide, and linguistic imperialism. Though the former two disciplines are fairly new, there is an intersection that exhibits synergies of oppression among marginalized racial groups. Using the range of emotions that the human heart is capable of expressing, writing has always been my confidante, a friend, somewhere to critique my flaws or celebrate my joys. Words have been the place where I harbor my deepest pain and my most cherished delights. Words are part of who I am, and in many ways, I believe, why I am.

As a social scientist, it is mission critical that I study society, social interactions among human beings, and their relationships. As a political scientist, I must extend this to the vast landscape of analysis of political trends related to human relationships through policies, legislative practices, and trends. As a Black woman, immigrant, and linguist, I take the unique intricacies and desynchronies of life to create a tapestry that impacts my lens and way of being. Imagine, then, a perfect circle of glass that is broken into the identities just represented; poetry becomes, for me, the glue that pieces them all together. Using this poetic landscape is my way to add my voice to the many creative, imaginative, and powerful voices in the research, scholarly, and literary world. Even more than that, it is my intent to make a scholarly contribution by applying what I have learned on the great journey of academic achievement to help paint a picture of understanding, knitting and connecting my experience as an immigrant, a Jamaican from the Global South, and a Black woman whose worldview is so different from the country I have been naturalized in. My epistemology shapes my frameworks, historically showing poems written from where I have been, my view in the moment of time that was poetically manifested, and who I am in the human condition with the collective experience of all those on whose shoulders I stand.

As a scholar, I am shaped by all those who walk the path of education and intellectual development and search for knowledge, and in my many sleepless, restless nights and waking hours, I am learning that all things are connected in a very delicate and intricate design that has to be traversed with care. As I am continually being molded and my thinking reshaped, these poems become an elevated way of interrogating the world and analyzing those things that impact us every day. Each has marked a milestone, pivotal moment, and transient juncture that has happened on a personal, local, national, or global scale, creating a shared experience with those with whom I co-identify, transcending the macro and micro levels of living and breathing civilization.

In my quest toward endarkenment, in the context of my growing understanding of being part of a global and fluid movement and continuum, endarkenment is to me the process of becoming African centered in my Afrocentricity. As I considered the first-edition subtitle, which was *A Quest Toward Enlightenment*, I discovered the word *enlightenment* did not quite fit with the process of higher consciousness. Not that anything is wrong with that word—in this sense, it just felt overused, as in everything light is good and everything dark is bad; as in the sense that the villain in every media representation is Black or Brown, or wearing black or brown, while the hero is blond-haired, blue-eyed, and wearing "light." I chose this title to beg the question, "Why not endarkenment?" so that this approach can be in conversation and interrogation of the positionality I took. "Afrocentricity recognizes our frame of reference so that we become the center of analysis and synthesis. As such, it becomes the source of regeneration of our values and our beliefs" (Asante, 2003, p. 51). To focus on the idea of endarkenment as a positive transformative process is to align my ideas with scholars such as Cheikh Anta Diop, who "refused to accept the idea that African history began when the Europeans became aware of it" (Asante, 2007, p. 33). Therefore, consider the creation ideology; historical developments of math, science, and language; the pyramids—if I truly believe that Africa is where these things originated, then how I view education is a process of endarkenment, not to discount or dismiss the contributions as noted through the hegemonic and Eurocentric concept or process of learning, but to accentuate and highlight the gifts and contributions that have made and built the foundation of Black-centered influences.

In learning about multiculturalism, Black consciousness, and politics, I am delving deeper into the "African-centered way" of thinking, and finding that it has given me a foundation and grounds to stand on. The positionality of being African centered is very much in line with the narrative and mission of the title. For me, to be African centered means that the lens I use to process information must first begin in Africa. Somewhere along the line, and in reviewing each of these poems, I discovered that I have always been Afrocentric. I'm passionate about who I am as a culturally diverse Black woman, an immigrant, and an American, which plays a vital role in my epistemological experiences. In this revelation of having always been Afrocentric and then later having learned what Afrocentricity is, it has dawned on me that this is also much of how I view the world and the framework by which I will use academic theory and method to extrapolate meaning and make sense of it all. This edition has evolved, and the subtitle of *A Quest Toward Endarkenment* has been removed to incite a fuller development of the original work by adding the new subtitle, *A Scholarly Poetical Science Discourse*. This, combined with my key interest in linguistic imperialism—as in the way words are used to strategically and intentionally keep people of color and people not of the imperialist race at a level of subordination—I felt adding a theoretical lens for each poem would add context to the experience. The theoretical lens to me would be the "scholarly discourse" piece that accompanies each poem, bringing in a deeper connection to social movements, political strategy, and legislative politics that have been powerfully weaponized. Movements such as Pan-Africanism, Black Lives Matter, Say Her Name, I Can't Breathe, and the emergence of "Karens, Kens, and Beckys" are significant current social and cultural events that impact not just our nation, in the way Black people coexist, but also our global ideologies in how we think of and interact with each other. These, too, add context that could live and breathe in the collective consciousness of those who turn the pages of this book—and in order to add to the scholarship that is so much more than myself.

THE COVER

For this second edition, it was important to me that the cover and content truly reflect the original intent of publishing this title. I absolutely love the cover of *Afrocentric Before Afrocentricity*, which is a dynamic reflection of the compilation within the pages, created with intentional listening and thoughtfulness. However, along with the content missing from the previous title was the academic component that did not fully evolve. The cover for A^2 is in discourse with the politics and lived experiences of social science, and it is my intent for this to be a more accurate manifestation of the scholarly poetical science rendition to the lens of research.

AFROCENTRICITY: ITS IMPACT AND IMPERATIVE

The Difference, The Disciplines, The Critique

Afrocentricity is not a process of counter-racism or hating another race in order to love one's own. On the contrary, it is a way, I believe, of loving oneself in order to truly appreciate all that others bring to our experiences. The superiority concepts of Eurocentric ideology—that have been the fundamental thought of all people globally—have negated the impact and contributions of other peoples and cultures. Afrocentricity brings attention to the assertion of African agency as different from Eurocentric individuality rooted and grounded in the particular experiences of Europe and presented to the world as Global Africa. What Dr. Asante (1988) believes is that not only must this belief system be amended, but for African people in the Americas, the Caribbean, and Africa, it must be transformed so that we are able to advance understanding based upon our own sense of agency. Calling for such a change may appear drastic, but "how do we prevent the creation and generation of mental enslavement and coloniality? This has to be one of the agenda items of African world philosophers. Too many Africans are agents of Europeanization, whereby they have taken on the race paradigm. One could argue that humans are free to choose a culture, but if one chooses based on abandoning one's own culture, it is human capitulation to the race paradigm" (Asante & Dove, 2021, p. 97). It is exciting to me, also, that one does not have to be a person of color or Black to be Afrocentric. Anyone can be Afrocentric, lending to the collaboration of allyship and co-conspirators.

There are obvious obstacles to integration as often demonstrated throughout history: the end of segregation and the integration of schools, which some believe have tampered the core of the African people—the Afrocentric belief that grounds us in culture. Dr. Wade W. Nobles (2023) writes, "The SKH as the science of the Being (Spirit) represents the ongoing struggle to free our thinking and practice from the constraints and limitations of Western orthodoxy and to rescue and refine African indigeneity as the praxis for the restoration of wellness with African American personhood, familyhood, and peoplehood" (p. 65), which for me expresses the loss of the glue in our belief system that holds the fabric of our culture together. To emphasize, he states that "embracing the SKH is an attempt to draw out the 'mindscape' or intellectual terrain that must be travelled in order to understand the core 'epistemic change' and 'paradigmatic shifting' necessary for the creation of a culturally congruent (Africa centered) program and praxis" (Nobles, 2023, p. 65). With this fundamental belief in mind, it is imperative to make a change in the educational structure of the *melting pot* called America, especially if it is to be that Black students excel.

> The "factory model" metaphor was trotted out so often that it became casually accepted as historical fact. "Our K–12 system largely still adheres to the century-old, industrial-age factory model of education," the then secretary of education Arne Duncan claimed in a 2010 speech. Similarly, the XQ Super School Project, underwritten by the extensive fortune of Laurene Powell Jobs, repeated the claim that public schools were relics of the past. (Strauss, 2020)

This discourse has been argued on both sides of the aisle, but it is very evident that there needs to be a deeper connection to culture and being for Black children to thrive. Many of the poems can be contextually understood by delving into the African philosophy of Dr. Théophile Obenga, Ubuntu psychology, and Afrocentricity, strongly grounded in poems such as "Queen" (p. 145), a resonant counternarrative, and "Named" (p. 117). Dr. Ronald Walters (2008) tells us that "the history of Black American oppression takes into consideration three categories of maltreatment that in the view of this author have maintained Blacks in a hole in relation to whites in American society until this very day. The first is slavery, the second is the extension of slavery and parallel forms of discrimination such as ghettoization, and the third is modern 'Black Codes'" (p. 78). "Black Codes" can be seen manifested prominently in many of the poems in A^2, as well as the poetical science discourse around them.

It is relevant to use the Afrocentric paradigm to shift away from the negative perpetuation of Black people in academic settings, political quips, and news media outlets aimed to sway the objectives of the population. Therefore, the Afrocentric paradigm is a tool used to realign subjectively and in conjunction with racial biases and discriminatory practices and provide a new way to assess the consciousness of the American culture in over 400 years of manipulation and suppression of people of color. "Under cultural imperialism, or what is referred to in this article as cultural oppression, the worldviews of divergent cultural and ethnic groups who share a common geopolitical space are unequally validated" (Schiele, 2005, p. 802). However, I stand with the paradigm, as expressed in the *Global Intercultural Communication Reader*, that "now, as an Afrocentrist, I approach the construction of knowledge from the standpoint of Africans as agents in the world, actors, not simply the spectators to Europe, since Afrocentricity constitutes a new way of examining data, and a novel orientation to data. It carries with it assumptions about the current state of the African world" (Asante et al., 2014, p. 104). Dr. Asante believes that this change must begin from the inside out, first with those who are recognized as African, Black, or African American, whether by their own intrinsic values, because they are categorized by skin color despite national origin, or thrown in for good measure due to the continued racial discrimination of the American culture. For even though

> there is discrimination in America toward other groups, such as Jews or Hispanics, Asians and Arabs, discrimination against Blacks has a different quality. But a comprehensive understanding of the nature of that victimization and its acceptance by the majority culture is suppressed by its own view of the condition of Blacks and its power to circumscribe the Black perception to a marginal role in the description of their own victimhood. The result is that Black victimization is still pervasive, in part, because a mythical presentative substitutes for the reality that continues to constitute this as a "qualitative" feature of Black life. (Walters, 2008, p. 79)

For centuries, the concept of the *glass ceiling* has been ingrained in the mind and mentality of African people and children; the long-term effects of enslavement are securely embedded in books and stories to maintain the hegemonic rule of the elite. The aim of Afrocentricity, used in this title, is to contextualize the poems as rooted in culture and in education. It is to emphasize the use of language as a stronghold across research and multidisciplinary studies. Words are the cellular structure that enables the function of all mankind, despite language. "Among Africans' reference for the word, based as it was on the future life, was the source of the Egyptian's concern with Ma'at and precision in language. You could not just say anything for emotional response; one had to speak truth as clearly as one knew how to do so. The appeal was not vile and obscene; it was measured and tempered with the quest for justice" (Asante, 2017, p. 7).

LINGUISTIC IMPERIALISM: A THEORETICAL LENS

Linguistic imperialism "focuses on how and why certain languages dominate internationally, and on attempts to account for such dominance in an explicitly, theoretically founded way. Language is one of the most durable legacies of European colonial and imperial expansion" (Phillipson, 1992, p. 1). Phillipson (1992) further explained that "imperialism has traditionally been primarily concerned with economic and political aspects of dominance. Later, theorists viewed linguistic imperialism as being more concerned with analyzing military, social, communication, and cultural activities, and the underlying structures and ideologies that link powerful countries" (p. 2). Language plays a pivotal role in politics and the dissemination of hegemonic priorities, which includes political ideological platforms; therefore, linguistic imperialism serves as an important lens through which to elucidate the discourse surrounding many political figures who use dog whistle politics to exact punishment and perpetuate the narrative of criminology to marginalized peoples. One of my most fun ways of interrogating linguistic imperialism is through reading texts like *Dog Whistle Politics* by Ian Haney López (2014), *White Rage* by Carol Anderson (2016), and my favorite, *White Fragility* by Robin DiAngelo (2018). DiAngelo speaks in a very self-intersective manner that is unusual, and challenges White people to reflect on their racist ideologies that they are quick to exempt themselves from. I invite you to read this book, but I draw to your attention this particular quote:

> The most profound message of racial segregation may be that the absence of people of color from our lives is no real loss. Not one person who loved me, guided me, or taught me ever conveyed that segregation deprived me

of anything of value. I could live my entire life without a friend or loved one of color and not see that as a diminishment or my life. In fact, my life trajectory would almost certainly ensure that I had few, if any, people of color in my life. (DiAngelo, 2018, p. 67)

I find this to be one of the most brilliant examples validating the framework of linguistic imperialism, because if a White person cannot even understand that their not recognizing the absence of others, or ever thinking for a second that it is strange that there is no one in their midst who doesn't look like them, is not okay, it is mind-blowing. Their privilege gives them the audacity to have the luxury to not care as long as they stay over there and we stay over here. For me, an African woman in America, it's appalling. Black people never asked to be colonized, raped, brutalized, and brought to parts of the world where they were the greatest means of commerce and most unvalued aspect of the communities they built. There are multiple layers to linguistic imperialism, like linguicism. Linguicism consists of "ideologies, structures, and practice which are used to legitimate, effectuate, and reproduce an unequal division of power and resources" (Ricento & Hornberger, 1994, p. 423). In discussions of race, feminism, and immigration, linguistic imperialism deals directly and indirectly with the concept of language. "Like racism, linguicism may be conscious or unconscious on the part of the actors, and overt or covert. It may be of an abstract kind (regulations for the use of particular languages) or more concrete (resource allocation to one language but not of others)" (Ricento & Hornberger, 1994, p. 423). Language and culture, as well as hegemonic power constructs, are defined, are redefined, and become culturally mutable based on the social value attributed to them within nations and nationalism. As the Republican base is conservative and has historically played to the diminished respect of other cultures and a disregard for contributions that immigrants make to the United States of America, it is not entirely surprising that Trump's outlandish mudslinging and undeniable racism have been so wholly accepted by the conservative party (Rosier, 2017). "Language is the blueprint of our realities. It is not *just words* that are emitted from our lips through a variety of sound vibrations. It is not characters etched on paper to infer or transpose knowledge or ideas. Language is the very fabric of everything that we think, live, feel, breathe, and do every day of our lives. No socially constructed race, color, creed, religion or ideology is immune from language" (Rosier, 2017, p. 199) or a structured form of communication.

Linguistic imperialism speaks to the ability to weaponize language as a means of subjugating other races and cultures, especially when it is directed toward people of color who were forcefully taken from their homeland and subjugated as less than human beings. In the case of Black people, who speak multiple languages and dialects and have a wide array of inflections, if being measured by the hegemonic race, they can be seen as inferior due to the differences in tone, cadence, and metric undertones. So what does this have to do with poetry, and why is poetry being used as a political science framework in this book? Easy. Not only is poetry words—an utterance in various tones, sounds, vibrations, languages, cadences, and learned behavior, used to express relationships between individuals, society, and the laws that govern them; Bourdieu (1991) tells us that "linguistic utterances or expressions are forms of practice and, as such, can be understood as the product of the relation between a linguistic habitus and a linguistic market. The linguistic habitus is a sub-set of the dispositions which comprise the habitus: it is that sub-set of the dispositions acquired in the course of learning to speak in particular context (the family, the peer group, the school, etc.)" (p. 17). Due to many of the psychological, behavioral, and lineage-related uses of language that create variation in verbiage, we have all experienced what we see in a broad expression of music across different cultures. Black music is distinctive, interwoven in a tapestry of color that is easily identifiable by that specific racial group. Same for poems, which in many cases are just music without the hook. Black poetry is very different from, say, White poetry. The structures are different, as in slam poetry. And though the poems written in this book would not necessarily be identified as slam, or distinctly Black, they are written by a Black woman, born and raised in the Caribbean, implementing my Jamaican lens and framework in a collision with colonialism and enslavement, from the worldview of an immigrant in the United States.

Many of the critiques of these poems come from the Eurocentric ideology that they have to fit into a certain framework of rhyme, limerick, metaphor, stanza, acoustic, ballad, elegy, ghazal, and so on. But if there are at least 150 types of poems, then poetry is poetry in whatever form it takes. Therefore, "a linguistic analysis and the analysis of literary critics, whose theoretical apparatus embodies such features as metaphor, symbolism, imagery, etc., may be said to strengthen reciprocally the conclusions arrived at by the different approaches. In addition to supporting the critical judgement of a poem's unity, the notion of coupling serves to explain a common exercise; namely, that poetry tends to remain in one's mind. Poetry has an enduring quality, and this not in the static sense of document or public property, by in the dynamic sense of individual recreation" (Levin, 1977, p. 10). Essentially, poetry is made of words for communication, and poetical science uses poetry as an analysis and literary criticism of politics and policies comprised of words, made into laws, that perpetuate the oppressive narrative of voice, sound, and language.

My research as a linguistic scholar came about for this very reason. I am intensely fascinated by the power of words, and how intricately they can empower or be weaponized. The "ideologies of language often appear to us as a form of common sense. They may even be quite invisible until they are carefully pointed out. But as we explore the possibility of political and economic interest in ideology, we find that 'common sense' has that status because it defines a group of people whose interests are advanced by believing in it, and not because it is necessarily true or even likely" (Hill, 2008, p. 34).

A^2, the title of this second edition, has given me a reprieve, a form of redemption. The first edition was published in my second year as a PhD student, and highly flawed. I had great big ideas as many graduate students do, and now later, with cumulative education, comprehensive growth, and continued learning, I am able to reassess and address much of what was left hanging. Growing as a political scientist, who experiences policies and legislative practices as a member of a marginalized community, provides me some additional context in focusing on linguistic imperialism. Having started out my creative career as a fiction writer and performance poet spitting in some of New York City's chic nerd spots, I have enjoyed the writing process of reading between the lines and drawing on the ambiguous and gray areas to tell a story. This greatly impacted my more structural learning as a scholar going through a dissertation defense process. As this lens of poetical science is new, I am sure there will be room to grow not just in this approach, but as a scholar. I revel in the metaphysical and psychological journey of digging to find the Black political scientist in me, being introduced to the free spirit that believes in the power of connectivity in the matrix of academia.

Additionally, much of the political strategy, discourse, and rhetoric used by print media, TV, movies, and video games helps to shape the collective consciousness of children; this collective consciousness, in turn, shapes lifelong adults who are impacted by everyday occurrences that will impact who they are at a very fundamental level. For this reason, poems such as "American Dream" (p. 31) and "It's Been a Long Long Time" (p. 93) are best given context by a corpus approach for analysis. Linguistic imperialism is the best framework for this book. "As Black women continue to experience issues and barriers related to the intersection of race, class, and gender, it is necessary to be able to identify a framework to study the multifaceted effects of these characteristics on women of color" (Chambers, 2023, p. 49). I draw on the ancestors, my community and networks, and the lived experiences of a little girl growing up in Brooklyn, New York, after migrating from Jamaica and learning the layers of words sociopolitically and culturally. I stand now as a forever learner, excited to experience and experiment with the educational process that I have attained as a researcher, and add to the discourse of those who have already paved a path with their blood, sweat, and tears.

REFERENCES

Anderson, C. (2016). *White rage: The unspoken truth of our racial divide*. Bloomsbury.

Asante, M. K. (1988). *The Afrocentric idea*. Temple University Press.

Asante, M. K. (2003). *Afrocentricity: The theory of social change* (Rev. and expanded ed.). African American Images.

Asante, M. K. (2007). *Cheikh Anta Diop: An intellectual portrait*. University of Sankore Press.

Asante, M. K. (2017). The fallacy of Trumpism: Donald Trump and the end of American political rhetoric: A contrast with ethical tropes in ancient Africa. In D. T. Harris (Ed.), *The rhetoric of Trump in essays and commentaries* (pp. 1–13). Universal Write Publications.

Asante, M. K., & Dove, N. (2021). *Being human being*. Universal Write Publications.

Asante, M. K., Miike, Y., & Yin, J. (Eds.). (2014). *The global intercultural communication reader* (2nd ed.). Routledge.

Bourdieu, P. (1991). *Language and symbolic power*. Harvard University Press.

Chambers, C. R. (2023). *Black women's pathways to executive academic leadership*. Universal Write Publications.

DiAngelo, R. (2018). *White fragility: Why it's so hard for White people to talk about racism*. Beacon Press.

Fenon, F. (2004). *The wretched of the earth* (R. Philcox, Trans.). Grove Press.

Hill, J. H. (2008). *The everyday language of White racism*. Wiley-Blackwell.

Levin, S. R. (1977). *Linguistic structures in poetry*. Mouton.

López, I. H. (2014). *Dog whistle politics: How coded racial appeals have reinvented racism and wrecked the middle class*. Oxford University Press.

Nobles, W. W. (2023). *Skh: From Black psychology to the science of being*. Universal Write Publications.

Phillipson, R. (1992). *Linguistic imperialism continued*. Routledge/Taylor & Francis Group.

Ricento, T. K., & Hornberger, N. H. (1994). Unpeeling the onion: Language planning and policy and the ELT professional. *TESOL Quarterly, 30*(3), 401–427.

Rosier, D. (2017). Linguistic imperialism: Trump and making America great again. In D. T. Harris (Ed.), *Newschaser: The rhetoric of Trump in essays and commentaries* (pp. 197–208). Universal Write Publications.

Schiele, J. H. (2005). Cultural oppression and the high-risk status of African Americans. *Journal of Black Studies, 35*(6), 802–826.

Strauss, V. (2020, December 11). No, public schools are not modeled after factories. Here's why Betsy DeVos keeps saying they are. *The Washington Post*. https://www.washingtonpost.com/education/2020/12/11/no-public-schools-are-not-modeled-after-factories-heres-why-betsy-devos-keeps-saying-they-are/

Walters, R. W. (2008). *The price of racial reconciliation*. University of Michigan Press.

RESOURCES

Ahuvia, A. (2001). Traditional, interpretive, and receptive based content analysis: Improving the ability of content analysis to address issues of pragmatic and theoretical concern. *Social Indicators Research, 54*(2), 139–172.

Anthias, F., & Yuval-Davis, F. A. (1993). *Racialized boundaries: Race, nation, gender, color and class and the anti-racist struggle.* Routledge.

Asante, M. K. (1980–1984). *The Afrocentric idea.* Temple University Press.

Asante, M. K. (2015a). *African pyramids of knowledge.* Universal Write Publications.

Asante, M. K. (2015b). *The history of Africa: The quest for eternal harmony.* Routledge.

Baker, M. (1991). Corpus linguistics and translation studies. In M. Baker, G. Francis, & E. Tognini-Bonelli (Eds.), *Text and technology: In honour of John Sinclair* (pp. 21–39). John Benjamins.

Bogle, D. (2014). *Toms, coons, mulattoes, mammies, and bucks: An interpretative history of Blacks in American films.* Bloomsbury Academic.

Deignam, A. (2005). *Metaphor and corpus linguistics.* John Benjamins.

Du Bois, W. E. B. (1994). *The souls of Black folks.* Dover Thrift Editions.

Duncan, G. A. (2007). Discourse, cultural imperialism, Black culture and language research in the United States. In G. A. Duncan (Ed.), *Discourse as cultural struggle* (pp. 143–154). Hong Kong University Press.

Esedebe, P. O. (1994). *Pan-Africanism: The idea and movement, 1776–1991.* Howard University Press.

Fernandes, J., Giurcanu, M., Bowers, K. W., & Neely, J. C. (2010). The writing on the wall: A content analysis for college students' Facebook groups for the 2008 presidential election. *Mass Communication and Society, 13*(5). https://doi.org/10.1080/15205436.2010.516865

Franklin, J. H., & Higginbotham, E. B. (2000). *From slavery to freedom: A history of African Americans.* McGraw-Hill Higher Education.

Gries, S. T. (2009). What is corpus linguistics? *Language and Linguistics Compass, 3*(5), 1225–1241. https://doi.org/10.1111/j.1749-818X.2009.00149.x

Jones, M. H. (2014). *Knowledge power and Black politics.* State University of New York Press.

Joseph, J. E. (2006). The social politics of language choice and linguistic correctness. In J. E. Joseph (Ed.), *Language and politics* (pp. 43–63). Edinburgh University Press.

Kaplan, H. R. (2011). *The myth of post-racial America.* Rowman & Littlefield Education.

Katznelson, I. (2005). *Wen affirmative action was White: An untold story of racial inequality in twentieth-century America.* W. W. Norton.

Ledford, K. (1998). English with an accent: Language, ideology, and discrimination in the United States by Rosina Lippi-Green. *Appalachian Journal, 26*(1), 46–49.

Loewen, J. W. (2007). *Lies my teacher told me: Everything your American history textbook got wrong*. Touchstone.

Mboutou, A. (1983). The Pan African Movement, 1900–1945: A study in leadership conflicts among the disciples of Pan Africanism. *Journal of Black Studies*, 13(3), 275–288.

Milhouse, V. H., Asante, M. K., & Nwosu, P. (Eds.). (2001). *Transcultural realities: Interdisciplinary perspectives on cross-cultural relations*. SAGE.

Mitchell, R. E. (1967). The use of content analysis for explanatory studies. *The Public Opinion Quarterly*, 31(2), 230–241.

Modiano, M. (2001). Linguistic imperialism, cultural integrity, and EIL. *ELT Journal*, 55(4), 339–347. https://doi.org/10.1093/elt/55.4.339

Nantambu, K. (1998, May). Pan-Africanism versus Pan-African nationalism: An Afrocentric analysis. *Journal of Black Studies*, 28(5), 561–574.

Perrow, C. (1967). A framework for the comparative analysis of organizations. *American Sociological Review*, 32(2), 194–208.

Pfeffer, H. E. (1976). Environments of organizations. *Annual Review of Sociology*, 2, 79–105.

Smith, D. L. (1984). Huck, Jim, and American racial discourse. *Mark Twain Journal*, 22(2), 4–12.

Stemler, S. (2015, December 2). An overview of content analysis. *Practical Assessment, Research, and Evaluation*, 7, Article 17. https://doi.org/10.7275/z6fm-2e34

Thompson, A. (1997). For: Anti-racist education. *Curriculum Inquiry*, 27(1), 7–44.

Walters, R. W. (1993). *Pan Africanism in the African diaspora: An analysis of modern Afrocentric political movements*. Wayne State University Press.

Wilder, C. S. (2013). *Ebony and ivy: Race, slavery, and the troubled history of America's universities*. Bloomsbury Press.

Woodson, C. G. (1933). *The mis-education of the Negro*. Tribeca Books.

PART I
Poems With Scholarly Discourse

CHAPTER 1
All About the Hair

Homegirl just wants to mess me over
Don't she know it's all about the hair?
My hair is tripping and badly needs a do-over
Before the dead decide to cross over in my naps
Chick got me walking around with the same homemade do
Drawing up a scare
And I know I can't say a damn thing because I just cannot go there
I am praying she don't mess around with my 'do
When a Black woman has to get her hair done
It's a sin what she has got to go through

This week I am still broke as hell
But I saved up the dough because I don't want to go through this again
Hair-raped and feeling a little down
My car needs gas
And I am broke and hungry
You know how we do, though, my hair is my priority
Talk all you want
You ain't gonna stomp on my ego
Taint my rep
Muddle my self-esteem—
Ain't gonna mess up the image of this here Black woman being presented as a dream

My hairstylist acts like she don't need my money
With five kids and no deep-pocket honey
How many appointments does this chick have?
Bump that, there's others
I don't want to wait
I swear this woman stirring up some serious hate
Visions of horror movies play out in my head like *Saw*, *Scarface*, *Mission Impossible*
With her in the starring role go . . . BUM!!!

Okay. That was kinda violent
Tired of stylists acting like they doing me a favor
Last time I checked, I was freakin' paying her

I need to have my hair done bad
And you know this stuff ain't cheap
My kinky, thick hair just don't cut it in the corporate world
And I need a job, for real
I ain't too picky
As long as I look like a bombshell
Just need some gel
Weave cascading down my back
Or some sewn-in curl
Gimme my foil tips
Some color highlights
Blond, rainbow, some real Indian, or "remy" synthetic waves—
Brazilian, Peruvian, or Malaysian
Don't judge me because my hair makes me look Blasian
Sewn in and bonded, you know they charge by the length.
This hair better last three months 'cause you know how much money I just spent
Kinky twists or perm
Yeah, I know I look good
Say what you want as long as I am tight under the hood

Tighten up my kitchen, girl!
Ooooh, I love my stylist. This chick can do some hair
Yeah, I recommend her; you got to go there
Sheen and holding spray, my finishing touch
Lemme get some lashes put in and makeup contour with some blush
Don't touch my hair
Or ask no questions
You know what time it is
I bought it so it's mine
Don't be ugly
Don't even go there,
Because when it comes down to it
It's all about the hair.

September 19, 1999

SCHOLARLY DISCOURSE

We are so used to reading stories of natural hair being "rejected in the workplace", that to be both a top professional and relaxer-free is almost unimaginable. (Black Girl Long Hair, 2015)

We now have documented information and research suggesting that weaves, wigs, perms, and other types of hairstyles for Black women are unhealthy. According to a recent report on braiders and those getting braids, then soaking them in hot water and/or coloring them blonde, these practices are causing reproductive issues in Black women, including cysts and infertility: "Black women across the United States are commonly exposed to carcinogens due to inadequate regulation of substances involved in hair braiding, an important cultural beauty practice. While public awareness of harmful ingredients in Black hair products has slowly been increasing, synthetic extensions as a source of toxins has not been an area of focus" (Thomas, 2023). Hair braiding is an option of wearing one's natural hair under extensions or fake hair for various reasons. Some Black women use it to protect their natural tresses, and others use it to get variation in style and color—many things they wouldn't do to their natural hair. Then there are other women who just like the "switch-up."

The scariest reason for wearing weaves, perms, wigs, and braids emerges when the Black woman is intimidated by the way society will view her and her natural curls, wrapped up in her appearance and possibilities. The workplace is one of the most toxic environments for women, who may feel they cannot wear their hair as it is because they will be subject to additional racism and discrimination on top of the already tremendous amount of stressors experienced on a daily basis due to being Black. Despite that, Black women should not have to die for their choices, become infertile, or have lifelong debilitating health issues that impact their quality of life. "In the Black Women's Health Study, 44,798 women with an intact uterus who self-identified as Black were followed from 1997, when chemical hair relaxer use was queried, until 2019. Over follow-up, 347 incident uterine cancers were diagnosed" (Bertrand et al., 2023). Unfortunately, this standard of self-hatred, and body mutilation in the form of hair manipulation, is not unique to Black women in the United States; rather, the standard expands deeply into the heart of the Global South and has remained there for decades. "A legacy of slavery, hair valuations reflect racially motivated beauty standards that work against Black females" (Robinson, 2011, p. 358).

Let's do a deep dive into the desperation for—and cost of—identity assimilation to look like the privileged race:

> There is plenty in history to show the struggles Black women (and Black men, too!) have had with acceptance of our Black hair textures. And, it's not just acceptance by others. We have long struggled with embracing the kinks, coils, and curls that grow beautifully, naturally from our scalps—a crowning glory and divine gift. (Samaroo, 2022)

In Africa, there are still huge banners on highways and byways advertising no-lye perms, long banned in the Global North. One scholar wrote that, out of their study, "it emerged that the reason for relaxing hair has little to do with emulating 'white' standards or copying ideals promoted in [the South African magazine] True Love; it is mainly associated with maintenance as most respondents pointed out that they relaxed their hair to make it easier to comb and style. In addition, some wear long hair for professional reasons, while others adopt long weaves to attract men" (Madlela, 2018). If the argument is that, in Africa, most of the women perm and weave their hair out of necessity and convenience, not self-hate, the narrative seems to be one of semantics. The very nature of changing one's hair by utilizing dangerous chemicals—in some cases, chemicals now restricted in Western countries—in order to find a man, and/or hopefully a professional opportunity, implies that Black (African) men find long weaved hair more beautiful than natural hair. Is it then not a fact that doing the opposite of one's culture, belief systems, and ideology is the very definition of internalizing the standard of beauty of White women who portray privilege and acceptance? What would happen if Black women decided to go natural? Wearing Afros is not acceptable or seen as beautiful, so Black women have begun to conform to the ideal of media and movies to look and feel the part of what is considered beautiful.

In light of some major advances in the support of Black women's hair, many are trying things like locs, ponytails, braids, and extensions—anything to avoid using perms, expensive weaves, and blond wigs. A report by Johns Hopkins University, that made it all the way to Jamaica, discusses that

> tightly pulling the hair into braids, dreadlocks, ponytails, or extensions raises the risk for what is known as "traction alopecia." The term refers to the gradual hair loss stemming from damage done during prolonged or repeated tension on the hair's roots. The study found that these types of hairstyles are common among African Americans, with about 33 percent of black women suffering from the condition. Among the styles at highest risk are braids, dreadlocks, weaves, and extensions, especially if chemically straightened hair is involved. Styles bringing moderate risk of traction alopecia include the use of wigs, permanent waves, and thermal straightening. Low-risk hairstyles include wearing the hair down, in loose buns, styles that avoid chemical relaxers and those that reduce friction on hair and scalp. (Korney, 2016)

This skepticism is not to dispute traction alopecia. It is indeed a real thing, and in the 21st century—when the human body is built differently based on diminishing resources, changing climate, and other behavior culpable in undermining health issues, like diet and exercise—traction alopecia plays a real role. But for context, it is important to note that Black hair was made to defy the ordinary. Historically, descendants of African cultures wore their hair in multiple styles that required pulling, sculpting, braiding, and even locs, and for centuries they were okay. The fear tactics of warning against the very hairstyles that provide options to Black women who want to veer away from the Eurocentric styles of beauty add to the fatigue of race identity. The fact remains that

> [i]n some ways, we are helpless in our obsession. Black hair became controversial as soon as our ancestors landed in America. Since then, we've been bombarded with images of the European standard of beauty—an image that was exactly the opposite of what our people viewed as beauty in Africa. Even in Africa these days, it's easier to find women with weaves and perms than natural hair. (Glanton, 2012)

Most Black girls from Latin America and the Caribbean have experienced the hot comb or the pressing comb. This was a painful means of burning the Black hair straight. The upgrade would be getting a perm, another dangerous form of straightening the hair in order to assimilate into the Eurocentric culture or ideology of Whiteness as the beauty standard. Today, according to the Jamaican *Gleaner*, "[a] trendy hairdresser who specialises in weaves ... explained that Jamaican women emulate the style of international celebrities" (Walters-Gregory, 2012). But even as they have moved away from that, their yearning for acceptance is quite palpable. Not that this is the fault of Black women; rather, it must be recognized that a system was set up for Black women to fail no matter what they did. The very existence of the Black body was cause for hate.

In addition to the health risk experiments that have impacted Black women and girls historically, the economic wealth and financial benefits are not flowing back into the Black community. Black women spend billions in the hair industry across the globe. "Some players in the beauty industry say they should be recognized for the contribution they make to Jamaica's economy" (Grant, 2016). But this is not just a Jamaican thing. According to one report, "the Black dollar was responsible for over $1 trillion in spending on consumer goods and services. Furthermore, Black Americans were responsible for 20% of all luxury goods purchases in 2021, even though we only represent 13% of the American population" (Christensen, 2023). Despite the food insecurities, poverty rates, and discrepancies in many of the low socioeconomic communities, Black people are sheltering the economy. Even in light of this realization, Black people do not spend in their communities at the same level of loyalty and protection that other racial demographics do. For those people from the community who wish to attempt to value loyalty, it is nearly impossible, because Black people are consumers and not creators of their own wealth. "That include[s] buying daily essentials from Black owned brands and reducing the money spent in other communities. [One Black filmmaker] chose to sleep on a park bench the night before a show after learning there were no nearby Black owned hotels in Athens, Georgia. He had soon come to realize that living completely Black is harder than it should be" (Marshall, 2020).

The fact is, even if Black people wanted to get into the retail business and benefit from the trillions of dollars spent on the Black hair care industry, it would be nearly impossible. Asians have cornered the market: "[B]ehind the beauty supply storefronts that dot the nation's urban neighborhoods and suburban shopping plazas sits a multibillion-dollar industry for black hair products that's run largely by South Koreans and does not cede its power or market share without a fight" (Sapong, 2017). The exploitation of Black hair in the beauty industry has made many

Asians wealthy, while Black women only have their kinky weaves and yaki hair bundles to show for the funding spent. Research has shown that within six hours the Black dollar leaves the Black community (Harrison, 2022); compare that to other communities where a dollar can last from three weeks to a month before returning to the U.S. Treasury.

Stepping into the sociocultural, political, and sociological concerns of demographic study written over three decades ago highlights the discrepancy between the need to reassess behaviors, priorities, and historical legacies and the measures used to perpetuate them.

REFERENCES

Bertrand, K. A., Delp, L., Coogan, P. F., Cozier, Y. C., Lenzy, Y. M., Rosenberg, L., & Palmer, J. R. (2023, December 15). Hair relaxer use and risk of uterine cancer in the Black Women's Health Study. *Environmental Research, 239*(1), 117228. https://www.sciencedirect.com/science/article/abs/pii/S0013935123020327

Black Girl Long Hair. (2015, January 21). 8 top professionals and CEOs who wear their hair natural. *Ms. Vixen.* https://www.msvixenmag.com/www.msvixenmag.com//2015/01/8-top-professionals-and-ceos-who-wear.html

Christensen, T. (2023, 27 February). *Op-ed: Respect the Black dollar.* MReport. https://themreport.com/featured/02-27-2023/respect-black-dollar

Glanton, D. (2012, August 25). Our hair-brained obsession. *Chicago Tribune.* https://www.chicagotribune.com/news/ct-xpm-2012-08-25-ct-perspec-0826-hair-20120825-story.html

Grant, R. (2016, 24 May). Hair! Hair! Beauty providers say they keep the economy spiky. *The (Jamaica) Star.* https://jamaica-star.com/article/news/20160524/hair-hair-beauty-providers-say-they-keep-economy-spiky

Harrison, I. N. (2022, December 14). *The lifespan of a dollar in Black community is only 6 hours: Fact or myth?* The Moguldom Nation. https://moguldom.com/430441/the-lifespan-of-a-dollar-in-black-community-is-only-6-hours-fact-or-myth/

Korney, S. (2016). *Dreadlocks, braids and weave could lead to hair loss.* Jamaicans.com. https://jamaicans.com/dreadlocks-braids-lead-hair-loss/

Madlela, K. (2018). *Black hair politics: The representation of African women on True Love magazine front covers and hair advertisements.* University of Pretoria Department of Library Services. https://repository.up.ac.za/handle/2263/65573

Marshall, K. (2020, October 1). *The Black dollar doesn't circulate like it should.* The Famuan. https://www.thefamuanonline.com/2020/10/01/the-black-dollar-doesnt-circulate-like-it-should/

Robinson, C. L. (2011). Hair as race: Why "good hair" May be bad for Black females. *Howard Journal of Communications, 22*(4), 358–376.

Samaroo, J. (2022). *How to embrace your natural hair: 26 famous quotes about Black hair*. Curly Nikki. https://www.curlynikki.com/2022/01/how-to-embrace-your-natural-hair.html

Sapong, E. (2017, April 25). *The politics behind the Black beauty store industry dominated by Koreans—MPR*. Shoppe Black. https://shoppeblack.us/black-beauty-store/

Thomas, C. G. (2023, June 22). Carcinogenic materials in synthetic braids: An unrecognized risk of hair products for Black women. *The Lancet Regional Health—Americas, 22*, 100517. https://www.doi.org/10.1016/j.lana.2023.100517

Walters-Gregory, S. (2012, January 30). Weaves: Trendy, fashionable and pricey. *The (Jamaica) Gleaner*. https://jamaica-gleaner.com/gleaner/20120618/flair/flair3.html

CHAPTER 2
All Woman

Being a woman is like being locked in a transparent ball,
A never-ending circle of no beginnings or endings,
And no one hears our call.
Being a woman sometimes feel like a rat trap
That cramps down on the very essence of our being
Taking us through living nightmares that men have never seen
We must be beautiful
Thin and tall
But the demands are endless
Because that's not all
Be poised
Stand straight
Pretty, pretty, pretty
Is a lady's pass through this life's pearly gates
Speak well
Be educated
Fight through this world or stand there naked
Naked of pride, integrity, and dreams
Leaving us void in our silent screams
Be polite
Don't talk foul
As if this world didn't teach us how
Be smart

Be witty
The perfect entertainment piece
And no one seems to care
That our pillow is our only release
Everybody's looking to go half on something
They want us to give all
And they give nothing
They want us to invest our hearts, our souls
The very essence of our being
They want us to take them places that they have never seen
Never mind paying
We must now take up the check
This is the '90s, girl, and I ain't finished yet
Be girlfriend, mother, family woman, and wife
If you can't be all
He thinks he's wasting his life
Best friends
Party girl
Career and pretty curl
Chest out
Tummy in
Remember thin, thin, thin
24 hours a day
7 days a week
Time just goes and goes and you still haven't gotten any sleep
Hold on to your seat, girl
The best part is yet to come
Because before the night is over
He's still gonna want some
This is where we must scream and pant
Melting from his touch
Because his fragile ego
Really ain't worth that much
With all this going on, trying to remember to breathe
The cycle of the circle closes in on us
And must still replant the seed

Being a woman is like being locked in a transparent ball
A never-ending circle of no beginnings or endings
And no one hears our call

January 23, 1999

SCHOLARLY DISCOURSE

Throughout history, women have been second-class citizens, and with every advancement (see Figure 2.1), women have been expected not only to celebrate the wins of their new place in society, but to still maintain the old ones as well. Coincidentally, some professions, once known as women's work, have become overwhelmingly saturated by men, causing the "underrepresentation in four predominantly female positions: nursing, elementary school teaching, librarianship, and social work" (Williams, 1992, p. 253), proving that while men may want women to maintain gender roles, they will unashamedly usurp them at will.

Politically, much like everything else, a woman's body has never been her own. Reproductive rights are determined by men, yet they are responsible for the vast lack of period products necessary for women and girls living under extreme conditions of poverty. Mortality for women and their babies is still high, even in First World nations, yet no one cares when data show that the recent banning of abortion in the United States is going to cause a significant increase in the number of deaths. "In the first year that all abortions are denied, some additional pregnancy-related deaths will not occur until the following year. Induced abortions (and thus abortion denial) commonly occurs early in pregnancy, but the majority of pregnancy-related mortality risk occurs late in pregnancy. Therefore, I estimate additional pregnancy-related deaths separately for the first year and for subsequent years" (Stevenson, 2021, p. 2023). This horrific prediction does not even include the deaths and mortality rates of Black women and children (Treder et al., 2023).

They do not provide proper housing or food (Hernández et al., 2016), yet they insist on banning abortions (Sherman & Witherspoon, 2024) or determining when, where, and how a woman can choose to have an abortion (Cohen, 2015), take the morning-after pill, and engage in other preventative health measures—all while pay equality is still at its worst for a woman doing the same job as a man. Despite all of these needs, from history to today,

> only rarely have feminists agreed on what they want the constitution to mean and then worked together to achieve their goal. From 1912–1920, they signed on to a campaign to pass a constitutional amendment and

thereby achieve the right to vote. And, from 1970 to 1982, they worked together for the ERA [Equal Rights Amendment]. Except for these brief episodes, feminists have disagreed over how to deal—constitutionally—with the issue of equality and difference. (McBride & Parry, 2016, p. 23)

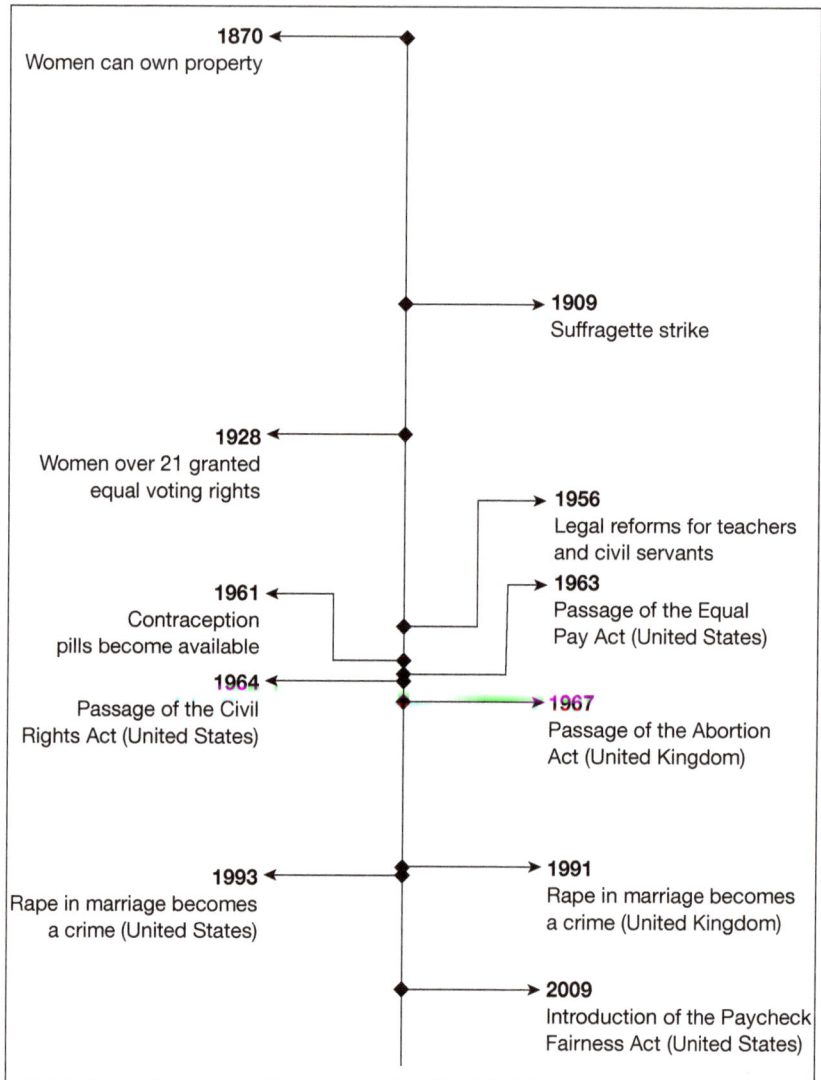

Figure 2.1 Historical Events Impacting Women

Sources: Adapted from "Gender and Income Inequality: History and Statistics," by G. Daugherty, 2023, Investopedia (https://www.investopedia.com/history-gender-wage-gap-america-5074898); "How Far Have Women's Rights Evolved in a Century?" by M. Molloy, 2018, *The Telegraph* (https://www.telegraph.co.uk/women/life/far-have-womens-rights-advanced-century/).

Men have not only dominated women's rights, but because most Eurocentric and Global North nations are patriarchal by nature, they have created the way women view, identify, reaffirm, and validate ideas, concepts of beauty, and lifetime expectations. One study used

> the metaphor of the panopticon, a particular prison structure that renders prisoners self-monitoring, [which] offers a useful way of understanding the mechanisms that inculcate an unrealistic body ideal in women. Foucault's notion of panopticism and a critical approach are used to show how textual mechanisms in two issues of *Shape* magazine—a women's fitness glossy—invite a continual self-conscious body monitoring in women. (Duncan, 1994, p. 48)

Within the layers of politically inhuman practices that induce cruelty toward them, women are leveraged for power play without their consent, and when—and if—they speak out, they are ostracized and shunned (Rochester & Heafner, 2021). Despite these unbelievable fiction-like treatments, women have found support, friendships, and ways to continue moving forward. Women are breaking barriers in senior leadership and executive roles (Ragins, 1998) and empowering other women to climb the corporate ladder, thus increasing wages and earnings. Women are the fastest-growing entrepreneurs and business owners (Brush & Cooper, 2012), refusing to marry, enjoying luxuries like traveling more, and refusing to have children (Traister, 2016). It can be argued that these last statements are justification for the banning of abortions and much of the political rhetoric more recently at play. In addition, they are justification for men feeling the need to protect the species and protect the race (Saletan, 2004)—in this case, the White race—and the growing fear of Afrophobia (Adejumo-Ayibiowu, 2023). On a global scale, the aging population of Japan (Jack, 2016), the lack of women in China due to the one-child rule (Cai & Wang, 2021), and the fertile, youthful population on the continent of Africa (Caldwell & Caldwell, 1987) are proving to be a contending motivation for the horrific practices toward women. Is it time to make a change? Is this the year of revolutions?

REFERENCES

Adejumo-Ayibiowu, O. D. (2023, September 7). The ultimate other versus the inferior other: An Afrocentric analysis of ethnic-stereotyping and Afrophobia. *African Identities*. Advance online publication. https://doi.org/10.1080/14725 843.2023.2250082

Brush, C. G., & Cooper, S. Y. (2012). Female entrepreneurship and economic development: An international perspective. *Entrepreneurship and Regional Development*, 24, 1–6.

Cai, Y., & Wang, F. (2021). The social and sociological consequences of China's one-child policy. *Annual Review of Sociology*, *47*, 587–606.

Caldwell, J. C., & Caldwell, P. (1987). The cultural context of high fertility in sub-Saharan Africa. *Population and Development Review*, *13*(3), 409–437.

Cohen, I. G. (2015). Are all abortions equal? Should there be exceptions to the criminalization of abortion for rape and incest? *Journal of Law, Medicine, and Ethics*, *43*(1), 87–104.

Daugherty, G. (2023, March 1). Women still earn less than men for comparable work in 2023 America. *Investopedia*. https://www.investopedia.com/history-gender-wage-gap-america-5074898

Duncan, M. C. (1994). The politics of women's body images and practices: Foucault, the panopticon, and *Shape* magazine. *Journal of Sport and Social Issues*, *18*(1), 48–65.

Hernández, D., Jiang, Y., Carrión, D., Phillips, D., & Aratani, Y. (2016). Housing hardship and energy insecurity among native-born and immigrant low-income families with children in the United States. *Journal of Children and Poverty*, *22*(2), 77–92.

Jack, D. (2016). The issue of Japan's aging population. *International Immersion Program Papers* (No. 8). University of Chicago Law School.

McBride, D. E., & Parry, J. A. (2016). *Women's rights in the USA: Policy debates and gender roles*. Routledge.

Molloy, M. (2018, February 6). How far have women's rights advanced in a century? *The Telegraph*. https://www.telegraph.co.uk/women/life/far-have-womens-rights-advanced-century/

Ragins, B. R. (1998). Gender gap in the executive suite: CEOs and female executives report on breaking the glass ceiling. *Academy of Management Executive*, *12*(1), 28–42.

Rochester, A., & Heafner, T. L. (2021). Retelling American history: Black women's resistance and fight for freedom, justice, equality, and cultural identity in the United States. *Theory and Research in Social Education*, *50*(1), 156–162.

Saletan, W. (2004). *Bearing right: How conservatives won the abortion war*. University of California Press.

Sherman, C., & Witherspoon, A. (with Glenza, J., & Noor, P.). (2024, January 12). Abortion rights across the US: We track where laws stand in every state. *The Guardian*. https://www.theguardian.com/us-news/ng-interactive/2023/nov/10/state-abortion-laws-us

Stevenson, A. J. (2021). The pregnancy-related mortality impact of a total abortion ban in the United States: A research note on increased deaths due to remaining pregnant. *Demography*, *58*(6), 2019–2028.

Traister, R. (2016). *All the single ladies: Unmarried women and the rise of an independent nation*. Simon & Schuster.

Treder, K. M., Amutah-Onukagha, N., & White, K. O. (2023). Abortion bans will exacerbate already severe racial inequities in maternal mortality. *Women's Health Issues*, *33*(4), 328–332.

Williams, C. L. (1992). The glass escalator: Hidden advantages for men in the "female" professions. *Social Problems*, *39*(3), 253–267.

CHAPTER 3
American Dream

What a hard life
Trying to make it in this world
It is so hard trying to just live and survive in Great America where stories of dreams coming true and streets lined with gold spread across the Caribbean like wildfire
I remember as a child when my father would visit
And how exciting it was to hear the stories of a place where a child can have their heart's desire
The sweet smell of want and hunger would burn our souls as gift-wrapped clothes and what-nots would come spilling out of a suitcase as sweet as perfume

I remember as if it was yesterday
Everyone adorning our foreign guests with respect and adoration
Holding them at high esteem as if on a pedestal
Wondering and shouting
"The Americans! The Americans!"
I would watch family
Related and unrelated
Beg, borrow, and steal their last dollar in the pursuit of an American passport or visa
And today as I remember
I wonder

Was it worth it?
Is it worth it to be here in a country where even being able to eat is a financial decision
When back in my country food grows in our backyards like weeds?

Is it worth it
To live in a country where even after achieving an education
A degree
One must still struggle with a job of minimum wage
Struggle to pay bills?
Where the thought of a smile is luxury?
In my country
Even in death there is a celebration of life
The elders tell stories of a duppy and Bro' Anansi on wooden, makeshift stairs at midnight
The playing of a song means to get up and dance
Back in my country
Our neighbor is our aunt and uncle and cousin
And the phrase "it takes a village to raise a child" has true intrinsic value

Is it worth it to live in this country
Where our grandparents are disrespected and put in homes
When back in their own country
They would be seen as wise
And sought out for their knowledge?

This country tells us lies
Tells us hard work is the true road to success
But how is that possible
When I see Caribbean people all over this country laden with depression and resentment?
When cleaning bedpans is the work of choice for a hard-earned dollar?

I remember as a girl
As a child with hopes and dreams
That this Great America was the answer to prayers

Chapter 3: American Dream

But their own lie in the streets like dust
With hunger in their bellies and dirty clothes on their backs
Their own cry for help, but the cries fall on deaf ears
And no one has time to listen
Yes?
Great America
The dream maker
What a life
What a lie

July 17, 2002

SCHOLARLY DISCOURSE

> The "intention" of White scholarship was to verify its grand narrative and scientifically demonstrate the actuality of its racially motivated or imaginary African American inferiority, that is, the diabolical dialectic. (Nobles, 2023, p. 23)

I still remember when family members would visit home from England, Canada, or the United States. Think of your favorite scent—fresh laundry, perfume, cut roses, early morning on a spring day, long walks in a summer garden; you name it—and that's what every single person exuded. There was no mistaking a "foreigner." The narrative from this piece has some components of what most immigrants might feel and think. The wishful thinking for a better life, the possibilities for opportunities, the chance to escape from persecution and torment... The list goes on and on, yet every immigrant's story is different and the same all at once. Taking into consideration the desire to escape, and the palpable yearning for the "American life," it should also be examined how it came to be that way. Dr. Wade Nobles (2023) speaks of the "White intention," which seems a fitting commentary on the historical theft, violence, and trauma that have pervasively infected every area of the globe inhabited by Black and Brown people.

> Europe had trained black men to wear those white masks which Franz Fenon wrote so bitterly about and which the racist culture of the United States would tear asunder. America was really the extreme example of Europe, stripped naked of all pretense about having a civilizing mission in the dark corners of the earth: a vast, energetic extension of the demonic Europe which the novelist Joseph Conrad had so maliciously identified as a Heart of Darkness in Africa. (Lamming, 1970, p. xli)

The disappointment, once only in the Global North, soon dawns on us all. Life in the Global South might be easier, in some sense, but the weight of the burden and the price are heavier. In some cases, it's a trade-off from one pain point to the next. The question must be asked: How did things become so dire all across the beautiful Caribbean landscape that escaping to a country like the United States—a land that has been so instrumental in the destruction of those who seek refuge in her bosom—is a better option? We have witnessed this so painfully in the massacre of innocent children being cleansed through genocide, hungry women lacking health care, and modern-day Caribbean citizens rushing for safety from natural disasters only to be struck down by those they look to for salvation. Aimé Césaire (1972) tells us that "it is not the head of a civilization that begins to rot first. It is the heart" (p. 48). It is the heart for compassion and empathy that reeks so much of evil every time we turn on the media or witness the pain of mankind even as American citizens line the streets like discarded litter, without the basics of human dignity. Though many people delight in its greenery, warmth, sunshine, and palm trees, others realize that the Caribbean's "spectacular beauty is matched by extraordinary diversity. There are volcanic islands which rise steeply out of the sea, their mountainsides covered with dense forest and scarred by fast-running rivers. There are coral limestone islands, flat, featureless and dry, where only cactus and scrub resist the heat. Some places are so fertile, it is said with some exaggeration, that a discarded match will sprout overnight into a tree. Others are rocky and barren, as inhospitable as desert" (Ferguson, 1999, p. 1). These contribute to a lot of the sufferation that has manifested as cause for concern.

So what is the Caribbean story? Why is it so ravaged and desolate despite the warm, clear ocean waters, filled with vibrant colorful sea creatures; despite the mountains so green and lush, trees so pregnant with delicious life-giving fruits and foods, and the people as diverse, pulsating and so alive, that the world over would swarm to its shores to discover what makes the Caribbean so great? People from the Global North (Meehan, 2009) love the music, the food, the dance, and the women, but sex tourism (Spencer & Bean, 2017) is a huge concern across the Antilles. The Caribbean is rich in natural resources, and yet, the Caribbean people have been reduced to paupers and beggars, scavenging for survival when they live in a place of plenty. Organizations that are set up to help the Global South, such as the International Monetary Fund (IMF) and World Bank, have instead failed the world (Burgis, 2015).

> Most Caribbean countries are burdened by large foreign debts, contracted during periods of economic expansion when their governments borrowed freely from banks abroad. The widespread economic crisis of the 1980's, which affected every territory, increased indebtedness as interest rates rose

and export earnings fell. Today, the Dominican Republic owes foreign creditors almost US $4 billion, while Antigua's 65,000 people are in debt to the value of US$327 million. Debt problems have required drastic remedies, and in the 1980's and 1990's Caribbean governments have turned to "structural adjustment" as a way of balancing the books. This has involved the widespread privatization of state assets to raise capital, the reduction of public sector payrolls and cuts in state spending on health, education and housing. The International Monetary Fund and World Bank have overseen adjustments programmes in most of the islands, offering loans in return for agreed economic reforms. The consequences have sometimes been explosive, as in Jamaica in the 1980s when devaluation of the Jamaican dollar and a resulting increase in prices caused riots and several deaths. (Ferguson, 1999, p. 329)

Much like Africa, the Caribbean islands have been left to fend for themselves after hundreds of years of plundering from the Global North, with nations like the United States filling their bellies while still the Caribbean citizens are hungry. Racial stigmas plague the ability of anyone of diverse heritage to make a way without sacrifice and compromise, who are still held as the sacrificial lamb of disgrace. Colonization, the division of the African continent for its natural resources, is the cause of the destruction we see today. The consensus comes from the fact that "the majority of whites instinctively disparaged the slave population, rationalizing the plantation system in terms of racial inequality. A mix of biblical and pseudo-scientific arguments was produced to justify African slavery, and planters, travellers and metropolitan pamphleteers consistently emphasized the alleged brutality and immorality of black people" (Ferguson, 1999, p. 108). The perpetuation of language narratives dehumanizing marginalized communities and its constant reinforcement by the privileged have solidified the concept of "colorblindness" to oversimplify the problem and justify the brutality. Capitalism and neoliberalism are the culprit, and institutions such as the World Trade Organization (WTO), World Bank, and IMF are making things worse, not better (Peet, 2003). Instead of facilitating opportunities for Caribbean and Global South countries to be sustainable, their mission runs counter, and that is to ensure they stay deeply in debt so that capitalism can prosper.

Many scholars have argued that there would be more equality if Africa was to become a sovereign continent and competitive among other nations. The methods of inferiority implemented have planted seeds and taken root in the core of the Black community.

> It is difficult to write soberly about the persistent influence of race in the formation of human thought. It holds a unique place in the consciousness of black people wherever they may be; and this is unlikely to change until

Africa becomes a black continent whose sovereignty is the product of her own institutions and is protected by an economic and military strength that can defy any intruder. (Lamming, 1970, p. xlii)

It is, in fact, difficult for the majority of demographics stigmatized as underprivileged and marginalized to soberly, without emotion, read, write, research, and share this truth. The ache is visceral, but the cure is within reach. Only our humanity can eradicate the virus of hatred and racial plague in this world. We just need to remember how to love.

REFERENCES

Burgis, T. (2016). *The looting machine: Warlords, oligarchs, corporations, smugglers, and the theft of Africa's wealth*. PublicAffairs.

Césaire, A. (1972). *Discourse on colonialism: A poetics of anticolonialism*. Montly Review Press.

Ferguson, J. (1999). *The story of the Caribbean people*. Ian Randle Publishers.

Lamming, G. (1970). *In the castle of my skin*. University of Michigan Press.

Meehan, K. (2009). *People get ready: African American and Caribbean cultural exchange*. University Press of Mississippi.

Nobles, W. W. (2023). *Skh: From Black psychology to the science of being*. Universal Write Publications.

Peet, R. (2003). *Unholy trinity: The IMF, World Bank and WTO*. Wits University Press.

Spencer, A., & Bean, D. (2017). Female sex tourism in Jamaica: An assessment of perceptions. *Journal of Destination Marketing and Management*, 6(1), 13–21. https://doi.org/10.1016/j.jdmm.2016.10.002

CHAPTER 4
The Broken Bridge

The bridge has been broken
Between the present and the past
History lost
The weight of our legacy trampled
Those who sacrificed
Those who died
Would roll in their grave to see the disregard—
To the broken bones
Beaten brows
Shattered dreams

The pain that has now been set aside—
As the past
Long ago
Teachers telling our children to forget
TV taking the place of books
Video games taking the place of kicking ball in the streets
Or playing in their backyards

The broken bridge
Where the future lay in suspense
Stranded in the middle not knowing how to move forward

With no recourse to going back
A movement lost when our children have no idea about the legacy
Of the shoulders on which their opportunities stand

A broken bridge of no hope
Lost dreams
Frustrated
Unstructured
Hopeless
Believing that the march and the noose were not about the rope around our necks
Believing that the singing of "Strange Fruit"
Is not about Black and Brown children dripping red like sand in the sea of forgetfulness
Standing in an abyss of nonsense
With no one to take up the baton and pass it on to the next generation
While Millennials and Gen Xers are astute at the game of—
"Put that down"
Or a shrug of "I'll pass"
Standing still in the present
Whining about the past staying in the past—

The broken bridge
Broken minds
Broken spirits
Broken people
Broken legacy
Broken time
Shattered!

April 1, 2015

SCHOLARLY DISCOURSE

Every year that something is written, it seems it might not be relevant the next, but sadly it is a social reality that more things are staying the same than are changing. "The Broken Bridge" reflects on how the pain of history has transcended the past to be a reality in our everyday lives. Today we are in a fight over semantics of good and bad. We are killing each other over ideology and socially constructed realities. Education has taken a back seat to those in power who wish to rewrite history and even the concept of feminism for women of all demographics; even White women are being attacked. Yet, even then feminism wouldn't consider women of non-White ethnicities, but that's a tale for another story. It is Vron Ware (2015) who said, "I am certain that the Girl Power rhetoric that was our intro to feminism covered everything but race and class" (p. ix). No one is safe. Most every scholar researcher from a marginalized group has questioned and furthermore summarized that the United States itself has racism built into its very foundation. It stands to reason that it is so difficult to confront something we cannot see. "Rather, the crucial constitutional issue in the area of racial equality today is whether the constitution requires or permits governmental entities to take account of the consequences of the long and tragic social history of racism in this nation that have created a condition of societal racial inequality" (Sedler, 1986, p. 677).

> The broken bridge
> Where the future lay in suspense
> Stranded in the middle not knowing how to move forward
> With no recourse to going back
> A movement lost when our children have no idea about the legacy
> Of the shoulders on which their opportunities stand

This paragraph is painful and frightening, because everyone's narrative is the same, but Whiteness is better, as summed in the text *White Fragility* (DiAngelo, 2018). Or we should overturn affirmative action so we can all be judged fairly on our merits (Montague, 2023), or we should ban books by anyone who is not White, heterosexual, and Christian, because we are one (Burgess, 2022). The confusion is palpable, and the intention to initiate fear is evident.

For those of us who live under the thumb of threats to our very existence, both overtly and covertly, obviously or subliminally, or narratives and rhetoric that those in power seem to think we do not notice or feel viscerally (maybe that is the intent), we are reminded of a few playbooks by those who support these narratives, and one of them is *The Willie Lynch Letter and The Making of a Slave* (1990). According to one title, "Cardinal Principles for Making a Negro,"

> For fear that our future generations may not understand the principles of breaking both horses and men, we lay down the art. For if we are to sustain our basic economy we must break both the beasts together, the nigger and the horse. We understand that short range planning in economics

results in periodic economic chaos, so that, to avoid turmoil in the economy, it requires us to have breadth and depth in long range comprehensive planning, articulating both skill and sharp perception. We lay down the following principles for long range comprehensive economic planning:

1. Both horse and niggers are no good to the economy in the wild or natural state.
2. Both must be broken and tied together for orderly production.
3. For orderly futures, special and particular attention must be paid to the female and the youngest offspring.
4. Both must be crossbred to produce a variety and division of labor.
5. Both must be taught to respond to particular new language.
6. Psychological and physical instruction of containment must be created for both. (*The Willie Lynch Letter and The Making of a Slave*, 1990, p. 12)

An additional principle of *The Willie Lynch Letter*, as well as other legislative practices that have perpetuated racial hierarchy and dissemination, constitutes the elimination of foreign languages.

One of the strategic cultural instruments that advanced capitalism deploys is linguistic imperialism. When this is successful, the dominant ideas can more easily penetrate the minds of the dominated, and the full development of other languages is forestalled, impeding the development of diverse counterhegemonies that are necessary for querying the rationality of monocultural, monolingual cosmology based on economic "efficiency." (Hamelink, 2000, p. 63)

To help bridge understanding, to help alleviate frustration, and to help dampen the weapon of hate and bridge the gap between those who are experiencing these ills through lived experiences and those who have always been co-conspirators (Hackman, 2015), we must speak truth to power. Fear is the sword being weaponized against us, sharpened by the lack of knowing, as all fear is. So let's continue to unravel the threads of history by never forgetting, through consistent "clapback."

We *must* continually contend with the legacy; without grappling with it, we only bind ourselves. Race is the one issue we are somehow supposed to address by not talking about it. But we must talk about it, and movements clashing over how to fight for a better future and deal with race as it is constructed in the United States. (Jordan, 2023, p. 91)

REFERENCES

Burgess, M. (2022, September 14). *Is banning books ever justified?* Forge Press. https://forgepress.org/2022/09/14/copia-de-book-banning/

DiAngelo, R. (2018). *White fragility: Why it's so hard for White people to talk about racism.* Beacon Press.

Hackman, R. (2015, June 26). "We need co-conspirators, not allies": How White Americans can fight racism. *The Guardian.* https://www.theguardian.com/world/2015/jun/26/how-white-americans-can-fight-racism

Hamelink, C. (2000). Human rights: The next fifty years. In R. Phillipson (Ed.), *Rights to language: Equity, power, and education* (pp. 62–66). Lawrence Erlbaum.

Jordan, B. E. (2023). Static: The illmatic consequences of the critical race theory boogyman. In W. G. Jerry (Ed.), *Illmatic consequences: The clapback to opponents of critical race theory* (pp. 91–107). Universal Write Publications.

Montague, Z. (2023, June 29). Inside the courtroom, justices exchanged divergent views of the ruling. *The New York Times.* https://www.nytimes.com/live/2023/06/29/us/affirmative-action-supreme-court

Sedler, R. A. (1987). The Constitution and the consequences of the social history of racism. *Arkansas Law Review, 40*(677). https://digitalcommons.wayne.edu/cgi/viewcontent.cgi?article=1127&context=lawfrp

Ware, V. (2015). *Beyond the pale: White women, racism, and history.* Verso Books.

The Willie Lynch Letter and The Making of a Slave. (1990). African Tree Press.

CHAPTER 5
Compelled to Be Silent

I have heard it said once of a King
That a Queen should close her eyes
Else the stars will fall and die
I have heard it said once of a King
That a Queen should relinquish noise and loudness
Whispers of surrender should sear her soul

I have heard it said once of a King
I have heard it said once of a King
And now I am compelled
To be silent

October 7, 2004

SCHOLARLY DISCOURSE

Since the rise of global capitalism and related ideologies associated with neoliberalism, it has become especially important to identify dangers of individualism. Progressive struggles—whether [they] are forced on racism, repression, poverty, or other issues—are doomed to fail if they do not also attempt to develop a consciousness of the insidious promotion of capitalist individualism. (A. Y. Davis, 2016, p. 1)

Throughout history, women have been considered substandard citizens in our culture and political environment. We have to stop the perpetuation where we "continue the strategy of silencing that keeps black men and women stuck, unable to engage the gender crisis in a manner that moves the discussion forward. There can be no constructive dialogue between black males and females about the gender crisis in black life as long as black men deny the reality of sexism and sexist oppression" (hooks et al., 1995, p. 5). Historically, men have received higher pay, better treatment, and respect despite women's equal footing in any career. Not only are we expected to be cute, cook, clean, and raise children, but we also must get jobs, be jolly, and be in a romantic mood when our men are enamored. The unfairness has been fought through feminist roles across the globe. However, when I reference the term *Queen* (Craig, 2002), I use it to recognize that, culturally, it is used liberally in the Black community when one Black woman wants to uplift another or recognize something unique or beautiful about her (Harris-Perry, 2011). However, this term falls on deaf ears, as Black women are subjected to harsh and inhumane treatment, especially when it comes to love. In song lyrics and pop culture, it is subjugated to being called out of one's name or paraded across the TV screen showcasing "mammy"-style entertainment of voluptuous curves coveted by other cultures but demonized and criticized when it's on Black women. The pain and ache of Venus's Hottentot resurfaces every time there is an exaggerated gawking at the Black woman's body (Gammage, 2016).

The "King" in this scenario, the Black man, has all but abandoned the Black woman as loud, abrasive, and not good enough to marry (S. M. Davis, 2017). Football players, basketball players, and even famous Black actors prefer to pass their wealth through marriage to those who are not Black, further handicapping the process of rebuilding generational wealth in the Black community (Galinsky et al., 2013). But while they prefer non-Black women for mates as they seek the designer baby or women placed on a sociopolitical pedestal, they do not want to see the Black woman do the same. As Black men in mass exodus marry White women or other people of color, the Black woman is once again left to either be alone or take what may be considered "rejects." If she chooses instead to find love among White men or other men of color, then she is seen as a sellout (Gonlin, 2023). She must toil and take the perpetuated narrative of her unworthiness and abuse. As not to perpetuate stereotypes, it is important to recognize that love is love. It is unfortunate that in a world of marginalization, where the social construction of race has permeated all facets of life, this simple human desire gets lost.

REFERENCES

Ani, M. (1994). *Yurugu: An African-centered critique of European cultural thought and behavior*. Afrikan World Books.

Craig, M. L. (2002). *Ain't I a beauty queen? Black women, beauty, and the politics of race*. Oxford University Press.

Davis, A. Y. (2016). *Freedom is a constant struggle: Ferguson, Palestine, and the foundations of a movement*. Haymarket Books.

Davis, S. M. (2018). The aftermath of #BlackGirlsRock vs. #WhiteGirlsRock: Considering the disRespectability of a Black woman's counterpublic. *Women's Studies in Communication, 41*(3), 269–290. https://doi.org/10.1080/07491409.2018.1505678

Galinsky, A. D., Hall, E. V., & Cuddy, A. J. (2013). Gendered races: Implications for interracial marriage, leadership selection, and athletic participation. *Psychological Science, 24*(4). https://doi.org/10.1177/0956797612457783

Gammage, M. M. (2016). *Representations of Black women in the media: The damnation of Black womanhood*. Routledge.

Gonlin, V. (2023). "Come back home, sista!": Reactions to Black women in interracial relationships with White men. *Ethnic and Racial Studies, 46*(10), 2020–2042. https://doi.org/10.1080/01419870.2023.2172353

Harris-Perry, M. V. (2011). *Sister citizen: Shame, stereotypes, and Black women in America*. Yale University Press.

hooks, b., Wallace, M., Hacker, A., Taylor, J., Bell, D., Reed, I., Hare, N., Williams, R., Caruso, C., Nightingale, C. H., Sleeper, J., Washington, E. B., Webster, Y., Tollett, K. S., Sr., & Brown, C. (1995). The crisis of African American gender relations. *Transition, 66*, 91–175. https://doi.org/10.2307/2935286

CHAPTER 6
Counternarrative

What they say vs. the truth

What they say vs. the truth about the statistics

What they say vs. the truth about the statistics of drug use by Black youths

What they say vs. the truth about the statistics of gun violence in the Black community

What they say vs. the truth about the lack of education among those Black and Brown

What they say vs. the truth about the contributions and positivity of the Black community in White America

The first lie that must be dispelled
Is that America has a White majority

The numbers don't lie

Yet the lie is perpetuated in everything but the truth

But the truth is hidden and told and reworded to hide what will lift the spirit and the mind

The noise would like us to believe that the Black and Brown man, woman, and child are the very sore to the core and the filth of life

The noise tries to say that drugs are sold and used by more and more Blacks every day

The story is told that more Black men are jailed than educated

The word is perpetuated

Propagated and instigated throughout the national news, by those who don't know
Those who don't want to know
Those who should know better
And those who take their news from those who should not be trusted
Yet, it is said that Black lives are worth more dead
That we don't contribute to the melting pot or the value of the American way
But still to this very day
No one will stand up and say
STOP!!!
The research has been done
That may have been the truth once, but that's been changed like the tide changes with the moon and sun
Can you hear me? SON!!!!
Black people walk the school halls and spit truth through the regurgitation of the institutional wall
We take the knowledge and the lies, and we reconcile that what needs to be done is to be validated by the minute some, who still control the strings of the puppet's tail
And we swallow as we wail
Watching lies unfold from the bellies of books
Without power to deny
We might sigh, but we march on until we can do different—

And different has been done
They can no longer say that we are the underbelly of the crisis when they have the guns
Shooting us down has become an epidemic when the rhetoric no longer works
But that's because we are living in the times of research
Technology putting the power in the hands of the poor
But they don't want us to have that no more—
So now they are trying to remove that by controlling the airwaves
Net neutrality is not a joke, and most of us don't even know what that is in order to invoke
Revoke
To fight

For the right
To the airwaves
But they are working on selling that too
Like water is becoming scarce due to the rich who pollute it so they can make poor people buy the very source of life
The bare essential to survive
Next will be the air we breathe
It may sound funny, but you won't laugh when they succeed

Don't believe me?
Go do your research
What they say vs. the truth is not a lie or an untruth
I am trying to save our youth
By saving the way we see each other
Think about our value
Or dream
Stealing our identity was just a small part of the strategy
It gets worse
When self-hatred has become so deeply embedded and there is nowhere to hide from yourself
Looking at each other we despise the very thing that reminds us of ourselves
The reflection in our brothers and sisters that should pump pride through our chest
And words of positivity from our breast to our lips to each other
Instead
We allow the lies to take root
But now it is time to uproot the weed of untruth from the garden of our minds
It is time
To read—
With headlines like "White America Does the Crime, Black America Gets the Time"
Just google it! It's online—
It's time to rewind
Time to unwind
Time to tell the truth

Time to reclaim the truth
Through counternarrative
Save our consciousness
And tell our own stories

January 31, 2016

SCHOLARLY DISCOURSE

The common strand in this piece is research. Already into my doctoral program, I had reached the understanding that narrative can be skewed to depict the image of the narrator—an idea that took hold and grew roots.

> There is an African proverb that says, "Until the lion tells the story, the hunter will always be the hero." It is our responsibility to share stories about Black History. Black History can be leveraged to unite and learn lessons, make equity commitments, and avoid repeating dark and oppressive behavior, attitudes, and actions. [Black History Month] can be used to celebrate the achievements of trailblazers in the past and the present. Black History is American History! (Detroit Public Schools Community District [DPSCD], 2021)

This quote from an African proverb (Mobe, 2022), along with the educational institution's intent to move away from the negative, is empowering. I chose to use this reference because it was diffused throughout the DPSCD. This is important to note because education is a pinnacle for disseminating misinformation, and the Detroit school district chose to empower its students to focus on doing research by reclaiming the narratives that have been perpetuated about who they are and their ability to excel.

> What they say vs. the truth
>
> What they say vs. the truth about the statistics
>
> What they say vs. the truth about the statistics of drug use by Black youths
>
> What they say vs. the truth about the statistics of gun violence in the Black community
>
> What they say vs. the truth about the lack of education among those Black and Brown
>
> What they say vs. the truth about the contributions and positivity of the Black community in White America

This piece was meant to hopefully shake the leaves of a tree so that a seed might fall and take root—a seed that will propel humanity to a place of justice and fairness. The misunderstanding of propagated information is powerful. It is so easy to fall into despair after watching the news or hearing that another person of color has fallen victim to the rhetoric of political commentary. In drug use, we know that "Black people are 24% of those arrested, but only make up 13% of the U.S. population—and people of all races use and sell drugs at similar rates. This arrest rate is instead due to targeted policing, surveillance, and punishment tactics" (Drug Policy Alliance, 2023). It is not unusual for "dog whistle politics" (Lopez, 2014) to be used in media and print publications that target the hegemonic demographic not just to believe this narrative but to implement those practices in communication and interaction with those who are victims of that rhetoric. The victims themselves are terrorized by self-hate, can and have internalized this societal bias, and even live up to it. Giving up and relenting to the loss of hope is part of the reason why we sometimes see behavior that seems to validate the narratives. Those who are wielding the weapon of words to justify and implement narratives that are codified to keep good people blind to these racist practices understand the power they hold in language. It is time to remove our blinders; if not of those who are weaponizing words, let's remove the blinders of those who are victims of it, by using counternarratives to reject false rhetoric and retain human dignity. Dr. Molefi Kete Asante (2015) asks, as I am asking now,

> Has it always been such a place where the true condition of African people are invisible and glazing over suffering, ignorance and cultural death allowed both Blacks and Whites pleasures like those of the burned brutalities, and dangling bodies from oak trees? Are we truly in a new world or merely the residents of the old one, awakened and frightened? (pp. 28–29)

For me, the answer is hope, collaboration, and remaining diligent toward the truth. It is this same drive that led the brilliance of Carter G. Woodson, Patricia Hill Collins, Stokely Carmichael, Cheikh Anta Diop, and the other revolutionaries who lay the path before us. We must keep moving forward.

REFERENCES

Asante, M. K. (2015). *The dramatic genius of Charles Fuller*. Universal Write Publications.

Detroit Public Schools Community District. (2021). *Black history*. https://www.detroitk12.org/cms/lib/MI50000060/Centricity/ModuleInstance/9703/black%20history.pdf

Drug Policy Alliance. (2023). *Drug war stats.* https://drugpolicy.org/drug-war-stats/

Lopez, I. H. (2014). *Dog whistle politics: How coded racial appeals have reinvented racism and wrecked the middle class.* Oxford University Press.

Mobe, T. (2022, May 23). *8 African proverbs that every global citizen should know.* Global Citizen. https://www.globalcitizen.org/en/content/africa-proverbs-global-citizens-action-end-poverty/

CHAPTER 7
Courting Through the Drums

Am I your friend?
Or are you courting me?
Because those are words that a man honors a worthy woman with
Words filled with passion and longing and questions that are answered and fulfilled only in the moment of truth
Words
Like painted lipstick on teardrop walls
Molding into and blending
The joining of images
Flashes of light that spark and ignite
Not just a fire
But a flame
A burning furnace that is the center of creation
Words
That is the beginning of creating
In the midst of what joins man and woman as one
Do you dare court a queen?
For then you must be willing to kneel

November 14, 2005

SCHOLARLY DISCOURSE

Why is there so much passive-aggressive interpersonal negativity among people? Why don't we just say what's on our minds and stop the games? The struggle for validity, to be seen, justified, and affirmed, is all wrapped up in the rising scheme of mental health and lack of sense of belonging in this world. Not only has this issue been rising over the past decade—suicide of the rich (Malone, 2018), the accomplished (Khan, 2024), and the poor (Hill, 2005) alike, people willing to throw it all away and then never look back—but it is a pandemic spanning geographic, racial, and educational acumen. I oftentimes wonder about the cause of such depths of sorrow and depression. Inexplicably, the rise in bullying, the trolling on social media (Hannan, 2018), the loss of sense of self in abusive relationships (Cantor & Price, 2007), and the lack of connection in courting rituals are grounded in something deeper than the individual identity of self. Where do we find cohesive discourse, synergy in communication, and sense of agency to self-advocate? The Afrocentric paradigm, the African-centered belief in community, and those who leverage the connection of family and legacy all lean into the call of culture.

As this poetic piece is about friendship, love, and relationships, I do not want to linger away too much from it. However, as the muse of scholarship would dictate its own direction, as scholarly discourse often does, I want to invite us at all levels to interrogate the conscious and historical manifestation of ancestral legacies and traditions as the common thread in all we do. In his foreword to Dr. Wade Nobles's (2023) pioneering text, *Skh*, Dr. Thomas A. Parham, president of California State University, Dominguez Hills, and a distinguished psychologist, writes:

> Dr. Nobles also reminds us all in this intellectual treasure, that understanding the essence of spirt is not simply a cognitive exercise but one that invites, if not demands, the use of sensation and perception as sentient beings capable of accessing and utilizing a full range of senses in coming to terms with what it means to be both truly conscious and human. (p. xi)

I stand with Baba Nobles and Dr. Parham that in everything we experience, being conscious of our humanity is pivotal. It helps to underscore the pain of loss, the trauma of bullying and trolling, and the sense of being abandoned and not belonging that have become so much a part of sociocultural diversity, equity, and inclusion efforts. It does not matter what position we hold; regardless of our accomplishments or riches, it is our conscious selves as humans that make the difference. What are friendship and love without character? What is family without history? What is community without a cause? This poem is not about overpowering each other, but about understanding that there are times each party in a relationship must submit, will come up short, or is lacking. This does not denote failure or lessen the value of a relationship. It is also not about 50-50 in any interaction because there is no such thing, and it is not about someone willing to die for you as much it is about loving someone so much that you wouldn't want them to. All the old wives' tales, ancestral adages, and cultural and spiritual belief systems lead from the same place: the power of the spirit, the strength of the collective, and the imperative of character. "The African and Native American world-view have similar cosmic concepts. Their intellectual traditions and thought-systems rest on the assumption of cosmic interrelationship" (Ani, 1994, p. 45). African griots and storytellers have all attested to the strain of forced enslavement, a disrupted history and trauma that has impacted the love within all of us. Could it be that the mixed messages, and lack of transparency in conversation, are a root cause of all this passive-aggressiveness, lack of communication, and transparent courtship?

Poetry and storytelling have always been a form of expression of the human emotion, and Verma (2017–2018) talks about the power of Maya Angelou's pieces that have touched upon our social, cultural, and political spaces so effectively. In the quest for Black love, she notes that some needs take priority other others, such as "the desire for motherhood, the desire for filial bonds, the desire for equal social respectability for the black woman and the overall emancipation of her community" (Verma, 2017–2018, p. 70). However, as you take on and interrogate this piece, "Courting Through the Drums," keep in mind that the inability to connect deeply might have been caused by the disruption of self. Nobles (2023) states that "our culture is our superpower" (p. 136). I invite the heart of the reader to find the strength of community and culture and the power of words to heal.

REFERENCES

Ani, M. (1994). *Yurugu: An Afrikan-centered critique of European cultural thought and behavior*. Afrikan World Books.

Cantor, C., & Price, J. (2007). Traumatic entrapment, appeasement and complex post-traumatic stress disorder: Evolutionary perspectives of hostage reactions, domestic abuse and the Stockholm syndrome. *Australian and New Zealand Journal of Psychiatry, 41*(5), 377–384. https://www.doi.org/10.1080/00048670701261178

Hannan, J. (2018). Trolling ourselves to death? Social media and post-truth politics. *European Journal of Communication, 33*(2). https://doi.org/10.1177/0267323118760323

Hill, S. A., Pritchard, C., Laugharne, R., & Gunnell, D. (2005). Changing patterns of suicide in a poor, rural county over the 20th century. *Social Psychiatry and Psychiatric Epidemiology, 40*(8), 601–604.

Khan, A. (2024, January 18). *Lincoln University of Missouri student affairs VP Antoinette "Bonnie" Candia-Bailey died by suicide.* Tech Ballad. https://www.techballad.com/lincoln-university-of-missouri-student-affairs-vp-antoinette-bonnie-candia-bailey-died-by-suicide/

Malone, S. (2018, June 8). *Celebrity chef, TV host Bourdain dies of suicide at 61.* Reuters. https://www.reuters.com/article/idUSKCN1J41JA/

Nobles, W. W. (2023). *Skh: From Black psychology to the science of being.* Universal Write Publications.

Verma, M. (2017–2018). Oppressed desire in Black women's narratives and its manifestations in Maya Angelou's selected poems. *Journal of Literature, Culture, and Media Studies, IX–X*(17–20), 68–74.

CHAPTER 8
Don't Hate Me

What is it about my Blackness that you hate?
Is it that you just cannot relate?
Is it that my Blackness makes you afraid to create
Or is it my creation that you just cannot translate?
My Blackness is rich like pure Black gold
Rich smooth gold that men have died for of old
A diamond powerful in its rarest form
That's me defined
But I mean you no harm
You look at my skin that's only a shell
But inside, you and I share and tell
We have the same fiber that makes us whole
We have the same knitting that men cannot unfold
Yet you look at my color
And choose to do me wrong
Life is a constant struggle of trying to be strong
Looking over my shoulder for what I cannot expect
Hate from my own brothers
I really cannot respect
Why do you hate me?
Is it something that I did?
The way I speak,

Act, or breathe?
What is it that makes you afraid?
My Blackness is really only just a shade
Look in my eyes and see what I feel
In them, you'll see the pain
I am afraid to reveal
Touch me and feel my soul
But don't hate me because you feel empty and out of control

July 11, 2002

SCHOLARLY DISCOURSE

This lamentation echoed throughout the Black community, a historical scar of what is experienced every day:

> We cannot continue to take our cues from beneficiaries or leaders who murdered, raped, castrated, whipped, beat, dismembered, and otherwise terrorized Black people between 1619–2022. Such notion is absurd, and yet we persist this way. We cannot continue learning from beneficiaries of Jim Crow. We cannot continue tolerating the perpetual degradation and humiliation of Black people, which has been taking place unexceptionally for more than 100 years (1688–1977). The period I am now referring to as America's 400-year Holocaust and Black Genocide involves cleansing this country of even any residue of Blackness that both slavery and Jim Crow did not destroy. We must all acknowledge, frame, and reframe White privilege, White power, and White supremacy as affirmative action for White people. (King, 2022, p. 27)

This poem, even now, evokes a range of emotions that weigh heavily as the political climate has seen a surge of violence and hate toward the Black body. Some of those emotions include sadness, frustration, nostalgia, and a sense of urgency (Essed, 2008). The imagery of a broken bridge adds visuals to invoke memory, a path between the present and the past.

This poem shows that there is an imagination of what could be possible or what was—a slice of nostalgia for the freedom childhood brought, overcast by ignorance and simply living. But in many cases where Black people live in the United States, it is easier to see pain and loss of innocence than bliss. The media is not kind to Black and Brown bodies; stereotypes violate the imagination and stifle dreams, and even then, hope is the bridge that fuels life. It's a wonder we still see people celebrating births, deaths, and marriages, all under the thumb of colonialist remnants that remind us that freedom is fleeting. But the human spirit is incomprehensible; there is always a longing for the disconnection between the past and the present in a time that seems stuck in limbo. Alice Walker (2006) wrote,

> This compassionate, generous, life-affirming nature of ours that can be heard in so much of our music is our Buddha nature. It is how we innately are. It is too precious to lose, even to disappointment and grief. Looking about at the wreck and ruin of America, which all our forced, unpaid labor over five centuries was unable to aver, we cannot help wanting our people, who have suffered so grievously and held the faith so long, to at last experience lives of freedom, lives of joy. (p. 93)

I suppose these words echo the aching that is bubbling up from this poem. The words echo what is manifesting in our political climate, which brought a level of fear into the anticipated future for Black people. Though hope is the string that ties us together, it is the forgetting that we struggle with, and we lament the lost traction made and the sacrifices of those who came before. I feel it now, as I did then, the expression of deep concern for the loss of historical awareness, the disintegration of cultural continuity, and the potential impact on future generations. "But while the West is engaged in a great debate about what it means to preserve culture, the indigenous world is aware that it has already lost the battle. It seems obvious to me that as soon as one culture begins to talk about preservation, it means that it has already turned the other culture into an endangered species" (Some, 1994, p. 4). This, for me, is a definitive reason to invoke the Afrocentric principle and urgency in the reclamation of the Black narrative through the urgent need for collective remembrance and understanding of Black history.

REFERENCES

Essed, P. (2008). Everyday racism. In D. T. Goldberg & J. Solomos (Eds.), *A companion to racial and ethnic studies* (pp. 202–216). Wiley.

King, D. D. (2022). *The 400-year Holocaust: Whtie America's legal, psychopathic, and sociopathic Black genocide—and the revolt against critical race theory.* Leadership DevelopME.

Some, M. P. (1994). *Of water and the spirit.* Penguin Group.

Walker, A. (2006). *We are the ones we have been waiting for: Inner light in a time of darkness.* The New Press.

RESOURCES

Ani, M. (1994). *Yurugu: An African-centered critique of European cultural thought and behavior.* Afrikan World Books.

Craig, M. L. (2002). *Ain't I a beauty queen? Black women, beauty, and the politics of race.* Oxford University Press.

Davis, A. Y. (2016). *Freedom is a constant struggle: Ferguson, Palestine, and the foundations of a movement.* Haymarket Books.

Davis, S. M. (2018). The aftermath of #BlackGirlsRock vs. #WhiteGirlsRock: Considering the disRespectability of a Black women's counterpublic. *Women's Studies in Communication, 41*(3), 269–290. https://doi.org/10.1080/07491409.2018.1505678

Galinsky, A. D., & Hall, E. V. (2013). Gendered races: Implications for interracial marriage, leadership selection, and athletic participation. *Psychological Science, 24*(4). https://doi.org/10.1177/0956797612457783

Gammage, M. M. (2016). *Representations of Black women in the media: The damnation of Black womanhood.* Routledge.

Gonlin, V. (2023). "Come back home, sista!": Reactions to Black women in interracial relationships with White men. *Ethnic and Racial Studies, 46*(10), 2020–2042. https://doi.org/10.1080/01419870.2023.2172353

Harris-Perry, M. V. (2011). *Sister citizen: Shame, stereotypes, and Black women in America.* Yale University Press.

hooks, b., Wallace, M., Hacker, A., Taylor, J., Bell, D., Reed, I., Hare, N., Williams, R., Caruso, C., Nightingale, C. H., Sleeper, J., Washington, E. B., Webster, Y., Tollett, K. S., Sr., & Brown,C. (1995). The crisis of African American gender relations. *Transition, 66,* 91–175. https://doi.org/10.2307/2935286

CHAPTER 9
The Evolution of My Child

This is the evolution of a child
Not the stereotype and propaganda that Black girls have gone wild
This child
She can flow from locs to Afro
Some lemonade box braids and not miss a beat in this summer heat
Yeah!
This child
The evolution of a child in the middle of a revolution
In the age of social media hysteria and cultural confusion
This child
Who will fight to resist
And strive to persist

Following the pursuit to a route
That seems to lead to a door of no return
But it is *this child*
Who will never question the beauty of her melanized skin
Because she knows pure Black gold flows from within
And she will dance
Not like there's no one watching
But because everyone is watching
As if the kaleidoscope of Black girls dancing is a sin

And there's some political win
When they kill our vibe
But she is resilient
Meant to survive
She will ride the wave of this transactional, ambiguous new rave
To not choose to fight
Because the right and the left are at war
As she comes of age
But
She is brave
Ready to free the world
She is strong
Diasporic knowledge keeps her grounded
In her ancestral song
She is Black girl rock
She is the evolution of a revolution
Dancing to the beat of the ancestral song
Kings lay so she can take her place on her polymath rock
From good stock
She is the budding queen
She will witness history
While telling her story as she writes
Filling blank pages
As she cocoons through the stages
Transcending time and space
Wisdom of Alkebulan shining and blazing
This is the evolution of my child

September 3, 2018

SCHOLARLY DISCOURSE

"The Evolution of My Child," originally titled "Happy Birthday, Cheyanne," is a poem that seems to encapsulate the feeling of a parent watching their daughter grow and change as the flow of life and time spurs her on to become someone free, aware, and resilient. Though I am not a parent, this poem speaks to me as I am a daughter and the subject

Chapter 9: The Evolution of My Child

of this poem. In my (short) time on Earth, life has been full of unexpected ups and downs punctuated by extremes in either direction. I think that everyone, including myself, strives to be able to better navigate the ebb and flow of living—to evolve and change for the better. As I have begun to better understand myself and the world around me, I have also had the privilege of deepening my understanding of my parents. From a daughter's perspective, it is interesting to see your milestones through the eyes of your mother, who's rooted for you and loved you your entire life. "The Evolution of My Child" describes not only a vision of what my mom sees in me, but what she aims for me to be. This poem creates a visual road map of sorts of my mom's dreams to see me nimbly traverse the complications of our broken society and break through the stereotypes that burden girls—especially the ones who look like me. Among those stereotypes, we find the pervasive notion of the "angry Black woman," which makes it hard for young Black girls to stand up for themselves.

> In the aftermath of slavery and the resulting social, economic, and political effects, Black women have become the victims of negative stereotyping in mainstream American culture. Such stereotypes include the myth of the angry Black woman that characterizes these women as aggressive, ill tempered, illogical, overbearing, hostile, and ignorant without provocation. (Ashley, 2013, p. 27)

It can be hard to understand this unconditional parental love—to hear what you feel was a stumble described as a steady, confident gait into the unknown. But that is the beauty of this poem: It tells us that as we learn, and grow, and change, there are people whose love for us will never diminish.

My mom, the author of these amazing poems, is one of the most important people in my life. She loves me, guides me, and inspires me. This poem, "The Evolution of My Child," though written for me, is an inspiration to me as well. It inspires me to push forward and embrace the uncertainties in life. It inspires me to question everything and to never doubt myself. And just like this poem inspires me, I know that it will inspire others. I know that not everyone is blessed to have a family as loving and encouraging as mine, but I believe this image of support can touch the lives of anyone who reads it. We are all metamorphosing and learning like a child does. There is no guidebook for how to live life, but when we have people who love us, their warmth can light the paths beneath our feet and show us that we are not alone.

As my mom wrote, this is an "age of social media hysteria and cultural confusion." The world seems to be changing at an alarming pace, and everything has become chaotic. In this era of "fake news" and individualism over collectivism, it can be easy to feel as though everything is falling apart. We find ourselves asking questions like "When did the well-being of us and those around us become so political?" An article in the *Journal of Experimental Psychology: General* answers that question by stating that

> [in this age] people engage in deliberation to protect their (often political) identities and to defend their preexisting beliefs. As a result, deliberation increases partisan bias . . . In the context of evaluating news, this means that increased deliberation will lead to increased political polarization and decreased ability to discern true from false. (Bago et al., 2020)

However, as we look to the future presented in "The Evolution of My Child," we know that if we band together, our collective strength can liberate us from the shackles that we impose on ourselves and that others impose on us. "The Evolution of My Child" is a wish for me, as my mom's daughter, and I hope to live up to the way I have been described. I believe that "The Evolution of My Child" is also a wish for all Black girls and women to strive beyond what society believes of them, and because of that I know this poem will positively impact the lives of people everywhere—parents and children alike. I am so glad that a poem like this exists, because it inspires, warms, and lightens the heart to where you don't just think you can do anything—you know you can.

—Cheyanne Rosier
BS, Cognitive Neuroscience, Carnegie Mellon University
MA, Animal Science (Film Thesis),
New York University

REFERENCES

Ashley, W. (2013). The angry Black woman: The impact of pejorative stereotypes on psychotherapy with Black women. *Social Work in Public Health*, 29(1), 27–34. https://doi.org/10.1080/19371918.2011.619449

Bago, B., Rand, D. G., & Pennycook, G. (2020). Fake news, fast and slow: Deliberation reduces belief in false (but not true) news headlines. *Journal of Experimental Psychology: General*, 149(8), 1608–1613. https://www.doi.org/10.31234/osf.io/29b4j

RESOURCES

Rosier, C. (2009). *Bumblebee longhorn needle*. Universal Write Publications.
Rosier, C. (2014). *Slayer*. Universal Write Publications.
Rosier, C. (2015). *Untamed*. Universal Write Publications.

CHAPTER 10
Follicle Affair

I've got a follicle affair with my hair . . . stylist
Hands so delicious I never want to miss
The way he drenches my hair, massaging me into bliss
Kneading and twisting
Pulling and tugging it tight
He's the only man to do my follicles just right

Tons of ringlets, my Black hair going from Afro to African locs
Naps clinging to his dark chocolate hands, my head is tingling like a burst of Tic Tacs
He takes passion in his duty, suds oozing through his fingers
I know when I get out of his chair I will truly be an Egyptian beauty

One step at a time, I hold my breath in anticipation
As he washes my wet tresses, dripping oils for my hair's rejuvenation
Just what it needs, he keeps me highly moisturized
Every pore in my head screams *Hallelujah!* as it's tantalized
Suds and bubbles get every itch down deep and strong
Sitting in this man's chair, I could never go wrong

Just when I thought it couldn't get more delicious
Pins and needles sticking into erotic subconscious
Blow drying . . . I am heated in ways that make me tremble
In anticipation of the final results
My Black tangles in adornment assembled
Looking in the mirror I am highly satisfied
With squeals of delight in ways I cannot hide
I have craved my appointment with the stylist of my hair's desire
Loving the way he sets my follicles on fire
Every yearning need is fulfilled with my hair
As I wait patiently to indulge again in our standing follicle affair!

March 2008

SCHOLARLY DISCOURSE

Who would have thought that Black hair would become a global conversation and a contentious issue in the United States? But when it comes to racism, nothing is off-limits, right? Though this piece originated as playful banter on the experience of going to the hair salon, a wash and shampoo is a luxurious experience for all. Let's talk about Black hair. Historically, in the African diaspora and across global Africa, Black hair symbolizes peace, love, war, beauty, storytelling, femininity, sensuality, culture, customs, religion, and nurturing (Montle, 2020). However, with racism came the demonization of everything Black and from the Global South (White & White, 1995). Eugenics theories and Whitewashing became the norm of Westernized societies.

> Europeans denigrated African religion both in the New World and in Africa. A barrage of derogatory treaties were written in Europe which called African religion ancestor worship, superstition, magic, fetishism and paganism. But the Bongo men who resurfaced were the product of African religion, the product of centuries of development and the accumulated experiences and ideas of generations. These religious and cultural experiences (developing independently according to region) were interwoven with religious ceremonies, rituals, and beliefs, and guided the evolution of customs. (Campbell, 1987, p. 25)

The truth is, however, that the function of supremacist beliefs and behaviors is toxic and contagious.

With all the attacks on Black hair (Luna, 2023), Black images (Rojecki, 2001), Black beauty (Millner, 2011), and Black agency, European culture and identity have ravaged the self-esteem of Blackness globally. Westernized media is unforgiving. "Music, music videos, imagery and television play a pivotal role in the messages individuals hear and see. These messages can be positive or negative, and they can influence how consumers and producers respond to and interrogate them critically, socially, physically, and emotionally" (Curtis, 2021). The attack has been systematic, instructional, foundational, and rooted so deeply that social science, cognitive health science, and medical science research is being done where Black children prefer to be White and non-Blacks fetishize Blackness and co-op, ridicule, or attempt to *be* Black in "unnatural" and "unusual" ways. It is almost frowned upon for a Black person to enjoy their hair at the level of contentment. If one has locs, as in the case of this poem, the Eurocentric view is that their hair is not washed, or that it is matted, or even that they do not go to the salon at all. If a Black woman wears her tresses in curls, an updo, or an array of styles, it is assumed that they are fake, a wig or weave. The idea that a Black woman can grow long hair or choose to wear it in an array of hairstyles is almost abhorred. After 1619 (Hannah-Jones, 2021), when Black people where claimed as property and subjugated to being not human but animal, their ability to fully embrace their agency as human beings and individuals was historically disrupted. As legalized enslavement took hold, Black people were "constantly reminded of their 'ugliness' and 'inferiority' to white people, [and] the black slaves began to believe the racist words of the oppressor" (Curtis, 2021). This began the process of self-hatred and intercultural persecution based on the ideology of beauty from a Western lens.

> With the arrival of Slavery, African Hair was seen as "Kinky", "Wooly" and unwanted which has been associated with the dehumanization of Slaves. This led to negative low self-esteem amidst Slaves and following generations leading to extensive "hair straightening" and also "skin lightening" which all reflected Black Self Hatred. ("Pre-Colonial African Hairstyles," 2023)

However, it did not stay that way. Black people have thrived and circumvented obstacles after obstacles. Lives have been lost, and the sacrifice adds fuel to the determination of survival. The push to tell the truth about Black people's history prior to 1619 has been energized. Social movements after social movements have ripped at the fringes of the fabric of democracy, tearing at the heart of Black humanity, yet the survival spirit of Blackness is unparalleled. Global Africa is truly a unique and dynamic continent to witness the amalgamation of so much diversity.

> As early as the 15th century, different tribes used hair to show one's social hierarchy. Members of royalty wore elaborate hairstyles as a symbol of their stature. Hair was also a symbol of fertility. If a person's hair was thick, long, and neat, it symbolized that one was able to bear healthy children. If someone were in mourning, they would pay very little attention to their hair. (Matshego, 2020)

African women and men have enjoyed the luxury of strong dynamic hairstyles that have been objectified and inspired many unsuccessful attempts at replication. In the United States, the Afro became the political embodiment of Black as beautiful.

> In *400 Years without A Comb*, Willie L Murrow explored the discovery of the Afrocomb in the late 60s which marked the first time Africans in the diaspora re-united with the most ancient hair care tool from before Slavery. The effect was a resurgence of Black self esteem with the rise of the Black afro-hairstyle and Black is Beautiful movement. ("Pre-Colonial African Hairstyles," 2023)

Civil rights took hold with media sensations such as *Good Times* (Heitner, 2013; Monte & Evans, 1974–1979) and *The Jeffersons* (Baptiste, 1986; Nicholl et al, 1975–1985). The 1970s donned Black beauties in Afros and their combs. The music was revolutionary, and the Black Panthers led the way. Continuing the spirit of precolonial Africans, it was a cultural embrace and reclamation of identity among Black people.

> Hairstyles that use natural Afro-textured hair belong to an ensemble of cultural practices. It is a fact known only to black people and those who regularly interact with them that letting grow, washing, unbraiding, combing, hydrating, and styling Afro-textured hair requires a lot of care and very precise procedures. In this way, there is nothing "natural" or—still less—negligent about these hairstyles. (Gordien, 2019)

Across the African diaspora, especially in the Caribbean, the locking of hair became a symbol of liberation and social movement. *Dreads* or *dreadlocks*, which they called themselves at the time, were a mixture of the anti-political stronghold taking part across the African diaspora, where Western countries have pauperized the people into legal enslavement. Those who rebelled were demonized.

> The obscene consumption and imitative nature of the petty bourgeoise provoked a cultural and anti-capitalist response from the youths who called themselves *Dreads* and who identified with the resistance of the Rastafari of Jamaica. (Campbell, 1987, p. 158)

Today, we have the CROWN (Creating a Respectful and Open World for Natural Hair) Act (Pitts, 2021). The U.S. military has changed their policies to allow Black women to loc their tresses as long as they can remain uniformed (Enokenwa et al., 2023), and Black hair is enjoying luxurious shampoo moments all over the globe. Though the world seems to have fallen into yet another social movement, and sometimes it feels like there is a time reversal at play, it is good to know that some things are unshackling the minds of Black men and women everywhere. Representation matters, and media anchors, military personnel, political figures, actors, writers, scholars, and all manner of Black people are showing up in spaces they have either carved out or knocked down the door to burst into; their visibility is setting the pace for the new generation of loc-livin', loc-lovin', and agency-reclaimed Blackness.

REFERENCES

Baptiste, D. A. (1986). The image of the Black family portrayed by television: A critical comment. *Marriage and Family Review, 10*(1), 41–65.

Campbell, H. (1987). *Rasta and resistance: From Marcus Garvey to Walter Rodney*. Africa World Press.

Curtis, J. (2021). *Black hair culture and vernacular visual language*. Design Enquiry. https://www.designenquiry.org/enquiries/2021/black-hair-culture

Enokenwa, M. G., Okoro, U. J., Cho, S., & Norton, S. A. (2023). Military grooming standards and Black hairstyling practices. *Military Medicine, 188*(7–8), e1996–e2002.

Gordien, A. (2019, September 19). *The Afro: More than a hairstyle* (M. C. Behrent, Trans.). Books & Ideas. https://booksandideas.net/The-Afro-More-Than-a-Hairstyle

Hannah-Jones, N. (Ed.). (2021). *1619 project*. The New York Times Company.

Heitner, D. (2013). *Black power TV*. Duke University Press.

Luna, J. (2023, February 10). *Hair discrimination and Black hair: What you need to know*. Political Fashion. https://www.political.fashion/posts/hair-discrimination-black-hair-what-you-need-to-know

Matshego, L. (2020, January 25). *A history of African women's hairstyles*. https://www.africa.com/history-african-womens-hairstyles

Millner, D. (2011, May 20). *The attack against Black girl beauty*. My Brown Baby. http://mybrownbaby.com/2011/05/the-attack-against-black-girl-beauty/

Montle, M. (2020). Debunking Eurocentric ideals of beauty and stereotypes against African natural hair(styles): An Afrocentric perspective. *Journal of African Foreign Affairs, 7*(1), 111–127.

Nicholl, D., Ross, M., & West, B. (Creators). (1975–1985). *The Jeffersons* [TV series]. T.A.T. Communications Company; NRW Productions; Ragamuffin Productions; Embassy Television.

Pitts, B. (2021). "Uneasy lies the head that wears a crown": A critical race analysis of the CROWN Act. *Journal of Black Studies, 52*(7), 716–735. https://doi.org/10.1177/00219347211021096

Pre-colonial African hairstyles. (2023, April 2). https://www.afrikaiswoke.com/pre-colonial-african-hairstyles/

Rojecki, R. M. (2001). *The Black image in the White mind: Media and race in America*. Chicago University Press.

White, S., & White, G. (1995). Slave hair and African American culture in the eighteenth and nineteenth centuries. *The Journal of Southern History, 61*(1), 45–76.

CHAPTER 11
Get Out of My Way

Get out of my way!
I said
Get the hell out of my way!
I will no longer listen to your lies
I will not allow you to creep into the crevices of my mind
And instill doubt and fear

Get out of my way!
Step aside
Because I have rested
I have prayed
And I have gained power
My spirit has been renewed
And I am no longer dying
My faith is my comforter
Hope has given me strength
And I am telling you that you are a liar
Get out of my way
You can no longer deceive me
Get out of my way
You can no longer control me
Get out of my way
I am an individual you can no longer send astray

You cannot tell me I am worth nothing
You cannot laugh at my frailty
Because I can laugh at you
I shut my heart and my mind to your stories
I will not let you plant the seed of doubt in my thoughts
My heart has been strengthened by a price long paid for my soul
I am at peace
And I have found my home
Blessings rain like sand on me
And I belong only to my Maker
So
Get out of my way!

December 30, 2002

SCHOLARLY DISCOURSE

With the rise of social media, we are constantly inundated with information about body image, money, who has what, and who has achieved more, not to mention bullying and cyberstalking, and it is easy to feel we are not good enough, we don't have enough, and we will never be enough. The psychological impact is devastating as more violence erupts, spilling over from the cyber to the real. "Some studies have indicated that social media use may be tied to negative mental health outcomes, including suicidality, loneliness and decreased empathy" (Berryman et al., 2017, p. 307). It can devastate us emotionally, taking a hit to our self-esteem and lowering our ability to withstand the internal battles to keep moving forward. The question is, then, "to what extent an improved awareness of the potential for social media to affect the psyche should actually be the conscious concern of all" (Brunskill, 2014, p. 391). There is so much more at stake than meets the eye—the general health of adults, for example, and the adults attempting to navigate the constantly evolving and emerging spaces on the interweb that serves as a distraction and disruption for the children within our care.

This piece is a reminder to stand tall, that we are wonderful just as we are, and that everyone's journey is different. So how does one stand defiant in the face of the intangible enemy—strangers we don't know seemingly doing better than we are, showcasing the best of their days, some hiding behind screens while their hearts bleed, and others looking to all of the self-proclaimed millionaire teenagers and young adults, waiting for you to take the bait so that you can be the catalyst for them to actually become rich? The list of naysayers (Dawson, 2018), negative comments, and horrors of possibly getting no "likes" is so powerful (Lee et al., 2020) that even finding the positive posts—the ones that are well meaning, the ones with real information—is like attempting to find a needle in a haystack.

Social media is not all bad, and not the only place where negative interactions can be a detriment to one's personal sense of self. Such negative experiences underscore our ability to process and negate interactions and experiences that could trigger our ability to "self-care" or send us spiraling into a bad space. That can occur at school (Vidourek et al., 2016), work (Williams, 1993), or play (Rubin et al., 2016). Sometimes these negative experiences occur at times when we least expect them and from complete strangers. How do we say "Get out of my way!" on steady feet, and how can we defiantly proclaim "I will no longer listen to your lies!" so we can truly be *at peace*?

There are effective and tangible resources that can help us affirmatively advocate for ourselves. According to Lavertue et al. (2002), ego-strengthening in psychotherapy is an option:

> Ego-strengthening may have many beneficial effects: improved therapeutic alliance, heightened insight on the patient's part, increased thought clarity, improved self-esteem, and shortened average length of therapy; it is thought that patients may not be willing to give up their symptoms until they feel strong enough to do without them. (p. 3)

Scholars suggest that self-advocacy can be achieved just by recognizing a social media troll—"It is important for healthcare professionals to learn how to spot a troll and the different strategies for dealing with them" (Dammann, 2019, p. 189)—and finding innovative and interactive ways to deal with workplace bullying before it gets out of hand (Kohut, 2008).

There is always a way to circumvent the stresses of life, to be fulfilled in our sense of self and well-being and not fall prey to the "likes," "clicks," and "shares" in spaces we cannot control. There are ways for us to combat these traumas without spiraling. We can all find opportunities that work for us. Whether you find it in yoga, self-defense courses, the gym, conversations with family and friends, brunching, travel, therapy, or meditation, there is a way for you to stand and tell anyone and anything who threatens your peace of mind, your process, mission, goals, and ambitions, to *get out of your way*. As long as your motto is to do no harm, and your mission is not to hurt but to thrive, there can be freedom, and there can be help.

REFERENCES

Berryman, C., Ferguson, C. J., & Negy, C. (2018). Social media use and mental health among young adults. *Psychiatric Quarterly, 89*(2), 307–314. https://www.doi.org/10.1007/s11126-017-9535-6

Brunskill, D. (2014). The dangers of social media for the psyche. *Journal of Current Issues in Media and Telecommunications, 6*(4), 391.

Dammann, C. M. (2019). How to spot and deal with internet trolls. In D. R. Stukus, M. D. Patrick, & K. E. Nuss (Eds.), *Social media for medical professionals: Strategies for Successfully Engaging in an Online World* (pp. 189–202). Springer.

Dawson, V. R. (2018). Fans, friends, advocates, ambassadors, and haters: Social media communities and the communicative constitution of organizational identity. *Social Media + Society.* https://doi.org/10.1177/2056305117746356

Kohut, M. R. (2008). *The complete guide to understanding, controlling, and stopping bullies and bullying at work: A complete guide for managers, supervisors, and co-workers.* Atlantic.

Lavertue, N. E., Kumar, V. K., & Pekala, R. J. (2002). The effectiveness of a hypnotic ego-strengthening procedure for improving self-esteem and depression. *Australian Journal of Clinical and Experimental Hypnosis, 30*(1), 1–23.

Lee, H. Y., Jamieson, J. P., Reis, H. T., Beevers, C. T., Josephs, R. A, Mullarkey, M. C., O'Brien, J. M., & Yeager, D. S. (2020). Getting fewer "likes" than others on social media elicits emotional distress among victimized adolescents. *Child Development, 91*(6), 2141–2159.

Rubin, M., Neria, M., & Neria, Y (2016). Fear, trauma, and posttraumatic stress disorder: Clinical, neurobiological, and cultural perspectives. In Y. Ataria, D. Gurevitz, H. Pedaya, & Y. Neria (Eds.), *Interdisciplinary handbook of trauma and culture* (pp. 303–313). Springer.

Vidourek, R. A., King, K. A., & Merianos, A. L. (2016). School bullying and student trauma: Fear and avoidance associated with victimization. *Journal of Prevention and Intervention in the Community, 44*(2), 121–129. https://www.doi.org/10.1080/10852352.2016.1132869

Williams, T. (1993). Trauma in the workplace. In J. P. Wilson & B. Raphael (Eds.), *International handbook of traumatic stress syndromes* (pp. 925–933). Plenum Press. https://doi.org/10.1007/978-1-4615-2820-3_78

CHAPTER 12
Halloween

There is a daily battle within me
Hating what they have meant to me
Despising what they are now
The hate saturates itself in the gravy of my mind and is marinated into disgust and passionate venom
I dream
But my dreams are haunted by a time where life was worth living
Taunted and teased by the evil of what life is today
Dreams of colors and vigor
Now drop like a dying flower
A cocoon of a butterfly that withers before it has earned its wings
Dreams die like the leaves of trees that once radiated with beauty and life
Leaves that slowly disappear from a tree that once flourished
Singing songs of glory in the rustling winds
My dreams have felt the blistering cold
Blanketed by the dull gloom of failure
Lost in a mirage of forgetfulness
Tainted by regret
Inside I am dying a painful death of knowledge
Where innocence dies and the truth of what is reality seeps through the cracks of the walls of happiness
Eating away at it like termites

Destroying the fabric of what was a stable foundation
Hate is my sword
Pain is my death
And tears
The relief and the release
The surrender
The acceptance of truth
Of wisdom
Knowledge that kills a soul
Hate that buries a heart
And pain that helps to forget
What happiness is

October 31, 2001

SCHOLARLY DISCOURSE

Psychology, the study of the human mind and behavior, derives from the Greek word *psyche*, itself rooted in its ancient African antecedent *sakhu*, essentially the "soul of being." It underpins the development of identity, personality, and consciousness. The study of the human mind and behavior cannot be separated from an exploration of matters of the spirit as they shape concepts of humanity and understandings of "self." Humans want to be loved and appreciated, and respected as they grow to understand the collective ideals from prebirth to adulthood. In this way, they can locate themselves, fulfill their potential, and contribute to their own and their society's future. (Asante & Dove, 2021, p. 37)

If what Dr. Asante and Dr. Dove say is true, then we are psychologically rooted in our existence to create interpersonal bonds. To be loved is at the very core of our soul, explaining why we have, as a collective of human individuals, shared variations of the same experiences. We have all experienced dissimilarities and aspects of the human condition. Some things are universal: illness, loss, success, triumph, birth, death, and heartbreak. Heartbreak covers everything except when we are happy, and it can come from anywhere. Asante and Dove (2021) go on to say that "culture will be used as the key to understand its powerful influence on human institutional development. While culture is essentially an anthropological idea, anthropologists along with explorers, biologists, linguists, historians, philosophers, physicians, theologians, writers, scientists, mathematicians,

... and others have been guilty of defining culture within a racialized hierarchy" (Asante & Dove, 2021, p. 35). In this case, it's nature versus nurture (Cross, 1990). Culture would explain why we do what we do, whether we are the receiver or perpetrator of pain on our fellow human beings. Culture is not about race; it's how we are conditioned to believe and value those around us. We protect what we value, and we mourn and lament the loss of what we value. Hence, psychopathy, hatred, and criminalized behavior are distorted manifestations of who we are as human beings. There is the love of lovers, siblings, jobs, parents, family, and friends, and each can manifest its own level of heartbreak and sadness.

Multiple levels of research discuss the intricacies of friendship, including how and what people do when a friendship has ended, which "have certain common characteristics. Sociologically, uncoupling occurs in a uniform way—a describable pattern. In order to uncouple, two people must disentangle not only their belongs but their identities. In a reversal of coupling, the partners redefine themselves, both in their own eyes and in the eyes of others, as separate entities once again" (Vaughan, 1986, p. 6). When those you trusted with your secrets, who were your confidantes, are no longer in your circle or there is a major betrayal, there are multiple levels of why, how, and who. Sometimes we see it coming, and sometimes we don't.

> Betrayal is when a friend, whom you counted on for support, love, affection, trust, loyalty, camaraderie, or respect, has somehow destroyed your trust. She may have violated a confidence or told a lie about you, harmed your personal relationships, or even cost you your job. He may have failed to come through for you in your hour of emotional need, taken your money, stolen the affections of your romantic partner or your spouse, or, in the worst-case scenario, physically harmed you or even caused someone's death. Were these "friends" ever really friends? (Vaughan, 1986, p. 6)

Whichever the scenario, we must realize that it can happen to anyone. Understanding the psychological and sociocultural underpinnings can maybe not heal the pain from the hurt, but can help us to navigate how we interact with others moving forward or, at the very least, provide some tools so it is easier to recognize red flags.

We often blame ourselves for loss and are unkind to ourselves. In some cases, we lash out and blame others. Sometimes we internalize the pain quietly, allowing it to fester, and sometimes we allow ourselves to grow, evolve, and move on. We have all heard a saying: Keep your friends close and your enemies closer. Why does this have so much appeal that it has stuck with us for so long? Others say to surround yourself with those who are like you in thoughts, words, and deeds—that being "equally yoked" is the key to having successful relationships—and this certainly rings true for the wise adage "birds of a feather." How we behave and react in adversity is no longer about nature, nurture, or culture. It is about character.

> Aesthetic ascriptions are always marks of approval or disapproval. Hence, ascribing aesthetic properties to particular people will depend on our relations. We are most likely, for instance, to find our friends and lovers aesthetically pleasing; our enemies aesthetically repulsive. Hence, one can treat the aesthetics of character only by venturing into the social context of these ascriptions—in this case, the field of human relationships. (Novitz, 1991, p. 207)

In some cases, such as David Novitz (1991) describes, we can dissect aspects of character and associate them with the "liking art" (p. 207), or how we feel about an individual. Though there are truths to this definition, it is very Eurocentric. From the African-centered perspective, the character is who we are in general (see Figure 12.1). It is not a choice. It

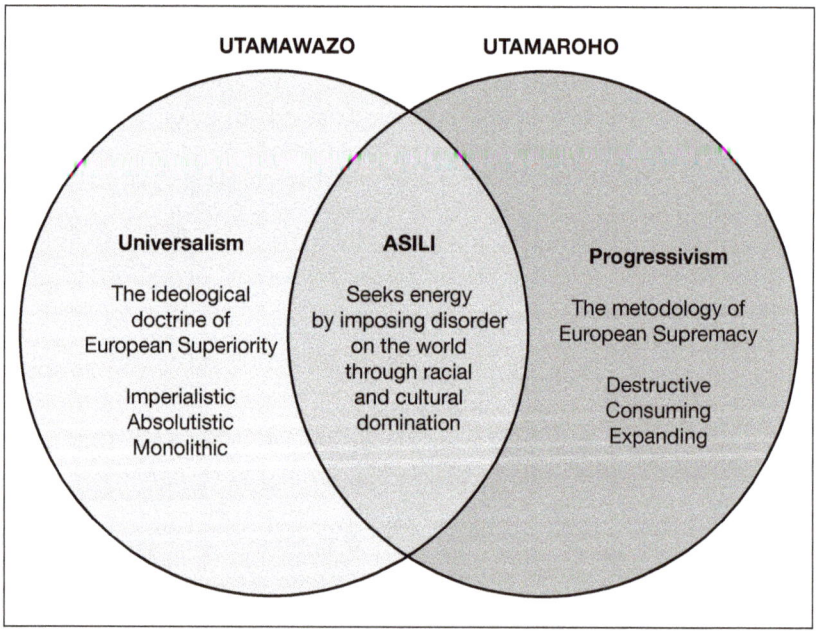

Figure 12.1 The Ideology of European World Domination

Source: Reprinted from "Book: *Yurugu: An Afrikan-Centered Critique of European Cultural Thought and Behavior* (1994) by Marimba Ani," by S. Winiger, 2019, Samim (https://samim.io/p/2019-12-30-book-yurugu-an-african-centered-critique-of-europea/).

does not matter if you think someone is good or bad; you will always do the right thing or strive to do the right thing because your character dictates it. It is not about whether someone is watching; it is not about what someone did or didn't do to us. It's about being authentic in everything we do. Ani (1994) describes this deep character reference as spirit, which "refers to the essential nature of a being. It is the idea that a person (or as it is in this case), a culture, or a group of people possess an immaterial (nonphysical) substance that determines their unique character or 'nature.' But the physical and nonphysical essence is there lined as it is in the concept of the 'gene' which carries 'memory'" (p. 15).

We have seen, heard of, and experienced, whether personally or by extension of our humanity, some individuals who are angry, passive-aggressive, or abusive (Cravens et al., 2015; see also Figure 12.2). We hear of violent crimes and divorces, and most people would wonder what makes a person do the things they do. The Enneagram-style image shown in Figure 12.3 points to some behavioral and personality attributes from which we can attempt to gain insight through communal sharing. But is it really up to us to figure these things out when we meet people, or is it our job as individuals to find safety away from what might harm us? "Self-blame refers to thoughts of blaming yourself for what you have experienced. Although inconsistent findings as regards the exact relationship have been produced, most studies have shown that an attributional style of self-blaming is related to depression and other measures of ill-health" (Garnefski et al., 2001, p. 1312). Suppose a man and a woman are in a relationship, and he is angry about his past failures. She must compensate for his lack of self-esteem and tolerate being barraged, attempting to prove she is different so he can stroke his ego and feel like a man (Forward & Torres, 1987). If your friends are thieves, they may claim to do no harm by unethically siphoning money from jobs or institutions because they believe it is owed to them or it won't be missed. If someone would admit these things to a stranger, gossip, talk behind one's back, or disclose personal intimacies or secrets, is the problem yours or theirs? There must be a sense of fulfillment for each person in the relationship; for it to last, there must be a sense of reciprocity, of being seen and heard (de Moor et al., 2021; see also Figure 12.4).

In Jamaica, there is a saying: There is a cover for every pot. This is true in all manner of relationships and all levels, so what might be for you may not be for someone else. And what you don't like might be a dream for another—a concept that has thrived in the success of thrift stores, farmers' markets, and garage sales. Knowing when to stay and when to let go is the key, but only we in our individuality can answer these questions for ourselves. Thinking about the sociocultural implications of human connections, it is best to consider how to move on and some tried-and-true ways toward healing and letting go. Fortunately, some competent experts are available in the fields of therapy, psychology, and mental health to attend to these questions.

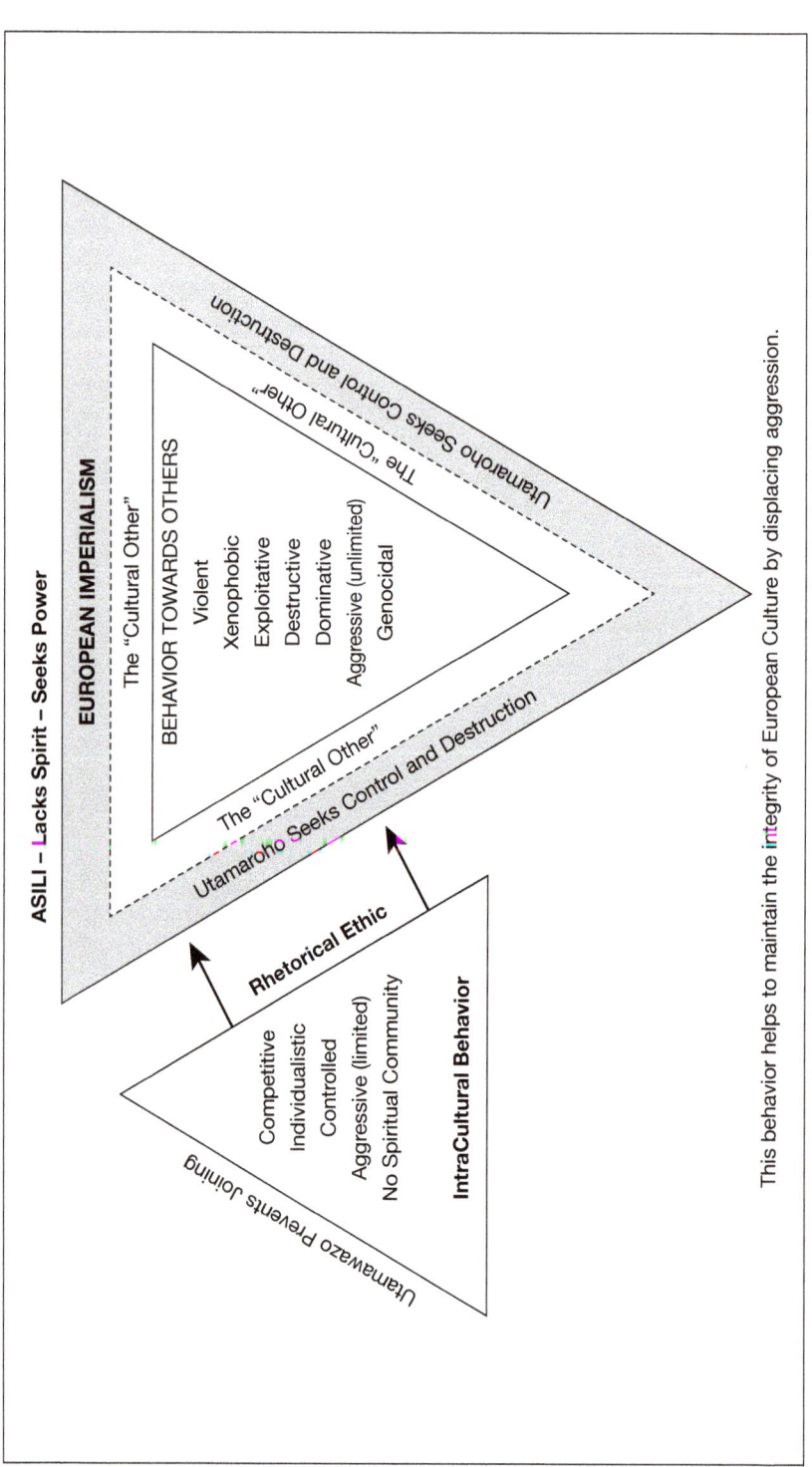

Figure 12.2 European Behavior and Ethics in Racial and Cultural Domination

Source: Reprinted from "Book: *Yurugu: An Afrikan-Centered Critique of European Cultural Thought and Behavior* (1994) by Marimba Ani," by S. Winiger, 2019, Samim (https://samim.io/p/2019-12-30-book-yurugu-an-african-centered-critique-of-europea/).

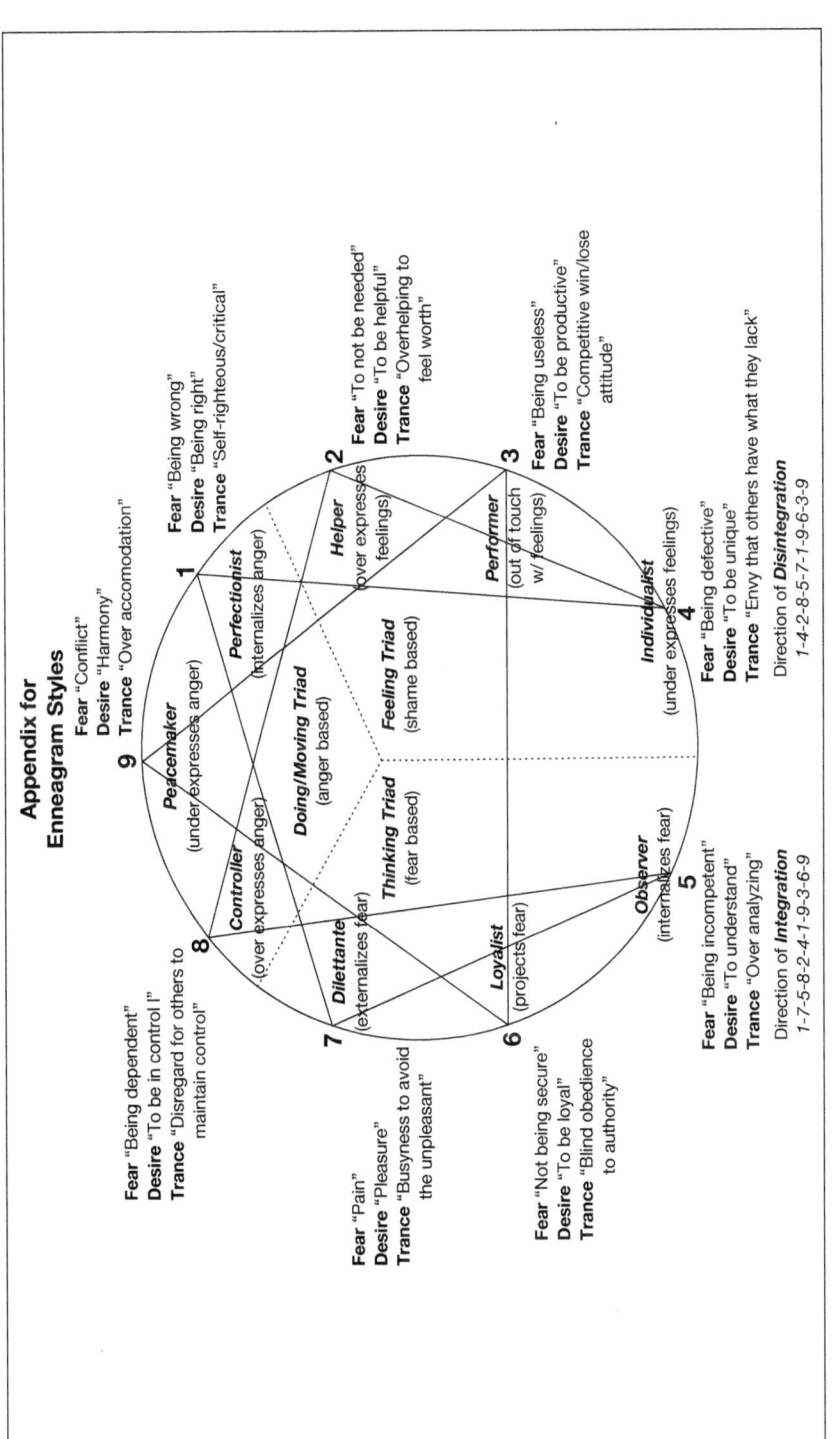

Figure 12.3 Behavioral and Personality Attributes

Source: Reprinted from "The Enneagram: An Enhancement to Family Therapy," by M. Matise, 2019, *Contemporary Family Therapy, 41*, 68–78 (https://www.doi.org/10.1007/s10591-018-9471-0). Copyright 2018 Springer Science+Business Media, LLC, part of Springer Nature.

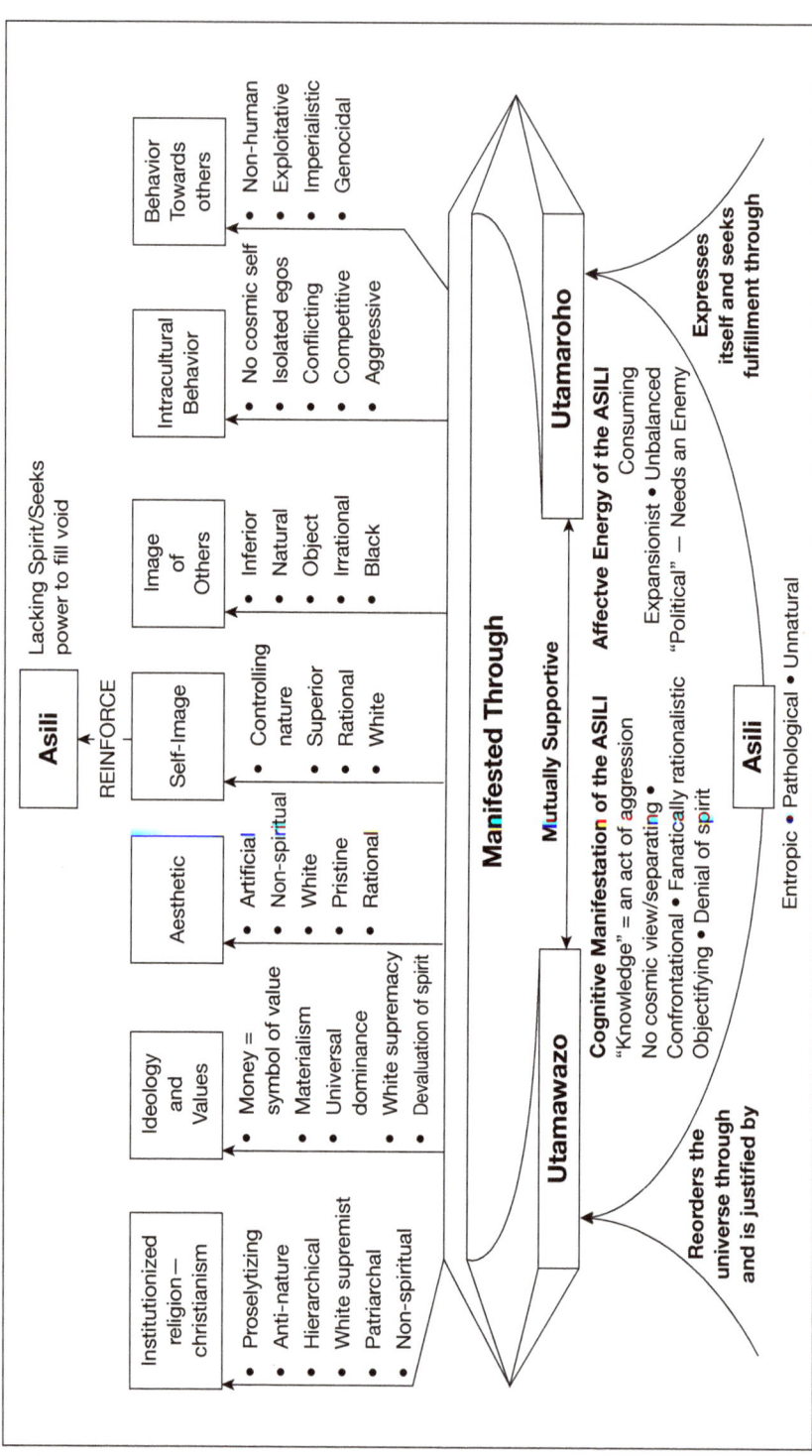

Figure 12.4 Tangle of European Cultural Pathology Creates System of European World Domination

Source: Reprinted from "Book: *Yurugu: An Afrikan-Centered Critique of European Cultural Thought and Behavior* (1994) by Marimba Ani," by S. Winiger, 2019, Samim (https://samim.io/p/2019-12-30-book-yurugu-an-african-centered-critique-of-europea/).

REFERENCES

Ani, M. (1994). *Yurugu: An Afrikan-centered critique of European cultural thought and behavior.* Afrikan World Books.

Asante, M. K., & Dove, N. (2021). *Being human being: Transforming the race discourse.* Universal Write Publications.

Cravens, J. D., Whiting, J. B., & Aamar, R. O. (2015). Why I stayed/left: An analysis of voices of intimate partner violence on social media. *Contemporary Family Therapy, 37*(4), 372–385.

Cross, N. (1990). The nature and nurture of design ability. *Design Studies, 11*(3), 127–140.

de Moor, E. L., Denissen, J. J. A., Emons, W. H. M., Bleidorn, W., Luhmann, M., Orth, U., & Chung, J. M. (2021). Self-esteem and satisfaction with social relationships across time. *Journal of Personality and Social Psychology, 120*(1), 173–191.

Forward, S., & Torres, J. (1976). *Men who hate women and the women who love them: When loving hurts and you don't know why.* Bantam Books.

Garnefski, N., Kraaij, V., & Spinhoven, P. (2001). Negative life events, cognitive emotion regulation and emotional problems. *Personality and Individual Differences, 30,* 1311–1327.

Matise, M. (2019). The Enneagram: An enhancement to family therapy. *Contemporary Family Therapy, 41*(3), 68–78. https://www.researchgate.net/publication/326093994_The_Enneagram_An_Enhancement_to_Family_Therapy

Novitz, D. (1991). Love, friendship, and the aesthetics of character. *American Philosophical Quarterly, 28*(3), 207–216.

Vaughan, D. (1986). *Uncoupling: Turning points in intimate relationships.* Oxford University Press.

CHAPTER 13
Her Name Is

I'm sure you know her
Or know of her—
The way she walks,
The way her radiant smile warms you like sunshine at each passing glance,
The way she treats you equally—
Whether her attitude is sunny or muggy and hot,
Whether she feels like raining or just being dull,
You have experienced her dynamic personality.
Were you ever taken aback by her uncanny beauty?
So phenomenal nothing compares—
The way her hips sway like the wind on a warm, windy day
How inviting and liquid the appearance of her lips,
Like the ocean
As it subtly yet powerfully washes up against the shores . . .
The way she speaks like a soft breeze
Calling, yearning, drawing you to her,
Whispering your name like soft cotton candy on a baby's tongue . . .
The way the mounds of her breasts curve and perk through the layers of fabric that cover her . . .
The smooth, touchable texture of her complexion, like ripe fruits,

Like nectar and peaches,
Inviting to the eyes
And succulently delicious to the senses . . .
The way her eyes seem to search you,
The way she showers you with compassion—everyone who knows her benefits from all she is . . .
Yet
She's miserable!
Hurting and torn apart inside
Why? Is that a glimmer of surprise in your eyes and disbelief on your face,
You who take her for granted and use her,
You who suck her dry of her natural beauty and resource?

Why do you look so puzzled?
You cannot see how one who lives to please
Can be battered so badly . . . She's weak,
Bruised and bleeding so profusely . . . She's dying,
You who rape her of her purity
And close your ears to her screams and pleas.
You deny what I say?
You do not recognize whom I speak of?
Her name is Nature
Mother Earth is her last name
Maybe now that you've formally met her acquaintance
You might be obliged to stop hurting her

September 5, 1994

SCHOLARLY DISCOURSE

We are living under extreme weather patterns. For decades, we have experienced extreme heat when it should be cold, extreme cold when it should be hot, and the disintegrating of microbes (Cavicchioli et al., 2019). Forest marsh areas are being destroyed and, with them, valuable wildlife (VanderMeer, 2023), all because of businesspeople overbuilding into our natural resources (Sochocki, 2023). Forests are dying, the ozone layer has thinned, and the results are extreme heath discrepancies colluding with a possible cause of the next ice age. "This question is not just of academic interest, to be debated by pipe-smoking professors at conferences. The rapid natural climate changes at the end of the Ice Age could be mirrored by man-made global warming in the 21st century, leading to devastating consequences for the planet's biodiversity and the human race itself" (Motavalli, 2023, p. 26). If this is not scary enough, food sources are diminishing, sea and land creatures are lost of their natural navigation, animals across the spectrum are wandering into areas of man for lack of food (Penteriani et al., 2019), and the changes to the ocean floor are making it inhabitable for the creatures who live there. There has been research around disappearing oysters and clams (Watson, 2015), for those who love to eat them, and the genetically engineered foods that once scared people have become acceptable forms of nourishment because the ability to produce natural foods has diminished (Dibden et al., 2013). There are insects that are invasive species traversing the globe and destroying those that have protected and pollinated areas of habitat (Mainka & Howard, 2010).

The National Oceanic and Atmospheric Administration (NOAA) has extensive research and information on their website. There are those who wish to deny the obvious, but it is clear that the problems and damage to Earth, hence Mother Nature, are due to human beings and the activities around industrialization, economic growth, and major inventions that continue to erode the planet. This poem was conceived so long ago, yet the threats have only increased. The pain and trauma enacted against Mother Earth, as described, are revealed by the personification of the Earth, feeling and experiencing what a person might, expressing a hope for inducing empathy and a call to action. So much is taken for granted just from living. There are complaints when it rains—something that can stop forest fires, fill reservoirs, and prevent the extinction of plants—because people wish to go out and party. They grumble that it's too hot, when the summer heat helps to bring forth new life, nurturing animals and pollinating flowers so they can be bought in stores, or appreciated. If it's too windy, or if it snows, there is never a time of complete satisfaction, yet we are aware that all these things must happen in their appropriate geographic region in order to sustain our mere survival.

While discussions around the issue are ongoing, "researchers found that more than a quarter of the world's population could experience an additional month of severe heat stress each year compared to the middle of the 20th century (1950–1979). High temperatures and drought could combine dangerously in places like the Amazon, increasing the risk of wildfire. In the American West, extreme fire weather will likely be more intense and last longer" (Tabor, 2023). In the United States, we are fortunate that

> President Biden created the first-ever National Climate Task Force, with more than 25 Cabinet-level leaders from across agencies working together on groundbreaking goals:
> - Reducing U.S. greenhouse gas emissions 50–52% below 2005 levels in 2030
> - Reaching 100% carbon pollution-free electricity by 2035
> - Achieving a net-zero emissions economy by 2050
> - Delivering 40% of the benefits from federal investments in climate and clean energy to disadvantaged communities (White House, 2021)

Scientists, and anyone with sincere concern for the Earth, were spectacularly pleased when the United States rejoined the Paris Agreement after a scary time of watching while the rest of the world, and much of the Global North, scrambled to find ways to lower the Earth's temperatures. The 45th president of the United States withdrew from an agreement signed by 196 nations with a commitment to climate change, turning a clear deaf ear to the fact that climate change is not just real, but "threatening our economy. It's threatening our future prosperity, the well-being of future generations" (Hersher, 2020). The agreement, which is a pledge to work together to lower greenhouse gas emissions, was resigned into law by President Biden (Cho, 2021).

And while deniers of climate change may scoff at the notion that it is possible that the world will end in disaster, it may have been happening so long that it's hard to believe anything will really happen. Either skeptics have increased, people do not want to know, or there is just so much selfishness, individualistic ideology, and greed. What cannot be denied is that there are those out there with the financial resources to build rocket ships in preparation for leaving the Earth if things get too bad (Dunn, 2021). None of these addresses poaching of exotic animals. Many children will soon be born watching television documentaries about the animals we take for granted today, because they will not be able to see one in real life. Zoos may one day, in the not-too-distant future, become a relic of the past. It is interesting to note that not all peoples or cultures are this nonchalant about the pending doom of humanity. There is value in and interdependence between man and nature in the Global South. Table 13.1 is an excellent example of the correlation between Earth and all those who live and coexist within it.

> African belief systems often outline concerns and care for the environment that may provide sustainability. African cosmology perceives nature as an interconnected system where all living and non-living things are interdependent. This worldview recognises the importance of preserving the

Plant Name	Scientific Name	Taboo	Belief
Mukumu	Ficus thoningil	Not to be cut	Hailstorm will fall and lightning will strike the perpetrator
Likhono	Chaetachme aristata	Not to be cut	The perpetrator's body will develop a rough skin
Mutsulio	Spathodea campanulata	Not to be cut	The perpetrator's body will develop a rough skin
Omuseno	Ficus exasperata	Not to be used as firewood	The smoke will lead to blindness
Isambakhalu	Boehmeria marc	Women not allowed to cut it	Will lead to miscarriage during pregnancy
Kukomosi	Maytenus hete	Not to be cut	Men and women in the family of the perpetrator will become infertile
Murave	Kigelia moosa	Not to be cut	The perpetrator's body will swell
Mulundu	Antiaris toxicaria	Not to be cut	Demons will attack the reaper
Musire	Croton megalocarpus	Not to be used as firewood	The smoke will cause blindness
Mukhomoli	Vangueria madagascariensis	Not to be cut	Evil spirits will attack the reaper

Table 13.1 Taboos to Conserve Trees in Kakamega Forest, Kenya

Source: Adapted from "African Belief Systems and Gendering of Eco-Justice," by S. M. Kilonzo, 2023, *Scriptura, 122*(1), p. 5 (https://doi.org/10.7833/122-1-2170). CC-BY-NC-ND 4.0.

environment for the present and future generations. African communities often rely on natural resources for their livelihood, and therefore, there is a strong incentive to preserve the environment. (Kilonzo, 2023, p. 3)

Much of the Caribbean also strongly depends on the environment and is connected to it as if one with nature. It provides for you, and you provide for it. This is the benefit of the African way and spirit, as far from

Eurocentric ideology as possible. Much of the Global South focuses on natural healing and medicinal practices that depend on unity with the Earth, and in "[W]estern culture, we don't even think of home treatment as 'medical care' (which usually has a sterile, professional, white coat-and-scrubs sort of connotation)" (Quinlan, 2004, p. 1). Without the Eurocentric images attached to it, most people think traditional medical and health care is insignificant. "As with any medical system, practice of bush medicine requires three-fold knowledge" (Quinlan, 2004, p. 2) in order to effectively use plants, fruits, trees, and other vegetation to impact healing in the human body. Today, for instance, what was once demonized as a drug in Western culture, ganja, best known as weed, is a celebrated practice among Rastafarians in Jamaica. "The use of ganja for spiritual purposes among African peoples is not without precedent" (Campbell, 1987, p. 109).

It is nearly impossible to discuss global warming, and climate change, without discussing the impact on health, food scarcity, birth rate and healthy babies both in humans and in animals, and the future for survival. They are all interconnected in intricate ways, pointing to the value of the African cultural behavior toward the Earth.

Scholars discuss the denial of global warming and the destruction of the ozone layer. Many conclude that there is both a fear of global warming and vaccine hesitancy. Despite the reasoning or justification, there are tangible evidence and obvious repercussions we must contend with, and hopefully, we can move toward averting this global crisis. As we are all aware,

> Climate change denial, like vaccine hesitancy, has a long history. The concept of global warming and greenhouse gases dates back 200 years to French mathematician Joseph Fourier (1768–1830). In 1820, Fourier reasoned that a fraction of the sun's heat energy was absorbed by the Earth's atmosphere, and acted like a garden greenhouse to keep the Earth's surface warm. If there were no greenhouse gases, Fourier predicted the Earth would be frozen. In 1856, amateur scientist Eunice Foote (1819–1888), and a little later, physicist John Tyndall (1820–93) discovered that traces of gases and water vapor did indeed absorb heat, and suggested that CO_2 may be responsible for the greenhouse effect. (Dobson, 2022)

With all the ways that this piece may be interpreted, it is hopeful that the call to action, the love of life and living, and the drive for survival will motivate more people toward the desire for collective action. Based on the National Climate Task Force's timeline of data (White House, 2021), this is not a new phenomenon, and maybe the challenge is that human beings have become desensitized to the global issue.

REFERENCES

Campbell, H. (1987). *Rasta and resistance.* Africa World Press.

Cavicchioli, R., Ripple, W. J., Timmis, K. N., Azam, F., Bakken, L. R., Baylis, M., Behrenfeld, M. J., Boetius, A., Boyd, P. W., Classen, A. T., Crowther, T. W., Danovaro, R., Foreman, C. M., Huisman, J., Hutchins, D. A., Jansson, J. K., Karl, D. M., Koskella, B., Mark Welch, D. B., . . . Webster, N. S. (2019, June 18). Scientists' warning to humanity: Microorganisms and climate change. *Nature Reviews Microbiology, 17,* 569–586. https://www.nature.com/articles/s41579-019-0222-5

Cho, R. (2021, February 4). *The U.S. is back in the Paris Agreement. Now what?* Columbia Climate School. https://news.climate.columbia.edu/2021/02/04/u-s-rejoins-paris-agreement/

Dibden, J., Gibbs, D., & Cocklin, C. (2013). Framing GM crops as a food security solution. *Journal of Rural Studies, 29,* 59–70.

Dobson, G. P. (2022, January 28). Wired to doubt: Why people fear vaccines and climate change and mistrust science. *Frontiers in Medicine, 8.* https://doi.org/10.3389/fmed.2021.809395

Dunn, M. (2021, July 8). *Billionaire blastoff: Rich riding own rockets into space.* Associated Press. https://apnews.com/article/spacex-lifestyle-travel-business-science-2a69d0fdf25907616a344b0729b6e7a9

Hersher, R. (2020, November 3). *U.S. officially leaving Paris climate agreement.* NPR. https://www.npr.org/2020/11/03/930312701/u-s-officially-leaving-paris-climate-agreement

Kilonzo, S. M. (2023). African belief systems and gendering of eco-justice. *Scriptura, 122*(1), 1–15. https://doi.org/10.7833/122-1-2170

Mainka, S. A., & Howard, G. W. (2010). Climate change and invasive species: Double jeopardy. *Integrative Zoology, 5*(2), 102–111.

Motavalli, J. (2023). The reckoning: Global warming is likely to cause huge climatic changes—and possibly a new ice age. *E, 14*(6), 26+.

Penteriani, V., Zarzo-Arias, A., Novo-Fernández, A., Bombieri, G., & López-Sánchez, C. A. (2019). Responses of an endangered brown bear population to climate change based on predictable food resource and shelter alterations. *Global Change Biology, 25*(3), 1133–1151.

Quinlan, M. B. (2004). *From the bush: The front line of health care in a Caribbean village.* Thomson Wadsworth.

Sochocki, T. (2023, June 1). *Supreme Court's wetlands decision could spell more construction, major impact on Florida.* WFLA. https://www.wfla.com/news/florida/supreme-courts-wetlands-decision-could-spell-more-construction-major-impact-on-florida/

Tabor, A. (2023, August 10). *NASA study reveals compounding climate risks at two degrees of warming.* NASA. https://www.nasa.gov/centers-and-facilities/ames/nasa-study-reveals-compounding-climate-risks-at-two-degrees-of-warming/

Vandermeer, J. (2023, July 12). Florida's environmental failures are a warning for the rest of the U.S. *Time*. https://time.com/6288683/florida-desantis-environment-climate-change/

Watson, S.-A. (2015). Giant clams and rising CO_2: Light may ameliorate effects of ocean acidification on a solar-powered animal. *PLOS One, 10*(6), e0128405.

White House. (2021, January 27). *National Climate Task Force*. https://www.whitehouse.gov/climate/

CHAPTER 14
It's Been a Long Long Time

It's been a long long time
It's been a long long time
Shackled by the memories of the past
We have institutionalized self-genocide
We scrub and rub and bleach as we despise the skin we're in . . .

[India Arie's tune]
"Brown skin,
You know I love your brown skin
I can't tell where yours begins
And I can't tell where mine ends"

Brown skin
From field hand to house niggah
We transition to alcohol in our communities
Feeding drugs to our own babies
We watch our neighborhoods and our neighbors wither and deplete
While the educated snobs climb the ladder of their corrupted versions of success
Tapping each other on the shoulder as they criticize and chastise how we have become a mess

It's been a long long time
But it's not so long ago that we can afford to forget
That we walk and talk on the shoulders of those who've been beaten down
Jailed
Because the world would rather forget
The signs on the water fountains from which our lips can be whet
We can't forget the revolutionaries who ignored
The detrimental travesties to themselves
As they walk the mortal line of pride
As they try to invest
Give their best
To us!

Yes, it's been so very long
We carry the burden so subtle
We tend to lie to ourselves
That we do this to ourselves
That instead of pulling up one's shoelace as Langston Hughes said
We become crabs in the barrel
And pull each other down instead

So so long ago
That educated people who look like you and me
Begin to crave all that we would once be lynched to . . .
Whistle at a who?
Beaten so badly and drowned
A 14-year-old Emmett Till grows up to be our present-day basketball and football stars
And we watch as they drown still
So long ago
We choose the wrong side of history as we cry foul
Screaming socialism like it's a bad word
Ashamed as if naked on the auction block
We hang our heads and 12 years a slave we are still looking back

Chapter 14: It's Been a Long Long Time

We turn away as we watch our blood struggle—
Shot in the head on crowded train platform
Immortalized now as Fruitville Station—
So we know the struggle is nowhere over
Much less to pretend it's dead

So long ago
That we think instead of bettering our own backyard and investing in ourselves
We're . . .

[*The Jeffersons* Tune]
"Movin' on up
To the east side
To a deluxe apartment in the sky"

Where we can mix and mingle with those who don't look like us
Don't like us
And still pretend sometimes not to see us
Until they do
Walking home with a hoodie and a bag of Skittles—
There is no difference between you and me and Trayvon Martin

So long ago
That I know some would even wonder as I recite these words
"What's the point?"
But I know it's just discomfort as we have perfected our . . .

Cover our ears, eyes, and mouth while saying
See no evil
Hear no evil
Speak no evil
Don't act like you haven't heard!

So so long ago
That every day we think we get better
Shattering myth after myth
As brown skin and blood now drip drip drip
Polluting
I mean diluting the vain idea of pure "I want to be like them"
On purpose
Instead of the days when wives and sisters were violated
Husbands and brothers give birth to the next generation of Uncle Toms

So long ago
That we fool ourselves into thinking
That my light brown skin is better than your dark brown skin
And with every glass ceiling we break
Barack Obama is still nothing but an *N*-word
And the hatred internal racial annihilation
Slaughter still perverts our lives
When instead of celebrating our accomplishments
We undermine all our beautiful Lupitas—
Yale-educated and Blacker than midnight glow—
My skin has never looked that ravishing!

Our children and the children before them
Are learning history from past-tense books
As images of Black holocaust disappear as fiction
Martin Luther King didn't look at his four little children and sacrifice his life so we can *talk* about change
Rosa Parks didn't sit down
So we can put each other down
The "Little Rock Nine" did not brave hate to integrate schools
So we can spit in their faces and drop out
The Harlem Renaissance is just a reminisce
Civil rights?
Slavery?
Reconstruction?
We forget so much we've been relegated to a month
As we stink and reek of self-destruction

Chapter 14: It's Been a Long Long Time

We forget that we owe our lives and opportunities to our ancestors
We trample their footsteps and scorn their memories
Turning the pages of *Who Was That Again?*
We forget that the "each one teach one" parable
Was not an exercise to enhance our vocal cords
But a fundamental principle

Raising hope out of the ashes of our lives
Some search for the dim light of the next generation of history makers
Ignoring the popularity paper rates
We are forced to remember that today is our history
Their very countenance is a contradiction
Faced with distance instead of celebrated as the evidence of growth
They climb the ladder of success
Teaching love through the hate
They break through the education cesspool
Of those who create discourse and keep discrimination institutionalized
Under lock and key because they are afraid that instead of being me I want to be *them*!

CRA-A-Z-ZY!
Our people border on the line of insanity
The journey hard and the road long
Whips and lashes still create psychological stripes on our backs
But we are destined to survive
Liberating our minds is the key
We must reach back for the hands of those who remember
Those who look like you and me
Those trying to remove the rope tied to our dreams
As we hang from the tree of deferred freedom
Yet we climb
They climb
Loosening the noose of . . .

"Strange Fruit" (chorus by Nina Simone)
And a crooning Billie Holiday
Shaking the tree as Black pain drips like memory
We bleed . . .

History remembers the glory
But making books with the agony of our ancestors is gory
And the whiplashing of our name
Is worst when it's slave mentality

But not everyone forgot
I didn't forget
I am forever stained by the blood of forget-me-nots
Knighted by the wisdom of truth
It's time that we take the mantle being passed to us
To carry the history and tell the truth

Because it's been such a long long time

March 6, 2014

SCHOLARLY DISCOURSE

The Legacy of Hate, Racism, and Homegrown Terrorism in America

It can be argued that America's greatest sin was not simply the enslavement of African abductees who became victims of international human trafficking to America as early as 1619, but the very act of racism itself, which existed before kidnapping became a catalyst for capture, bondage and oppression of African male and female children, youth, and adults brought to America. Racism allowed for untrue beliefs to become a significant part of an effort by those who subjugated other people to establish hegemony, which demonstrated a need to convey supremacy in domination and authority of power and control. The legacy of racism, hate and homegrown terrorism in America calls for an in-depth examination of the fact that racism preceded and inspired almost four centuries of intense personal and institutional cruelty and brutality throughout both the slave trade, as well as the eradication of Native American Indian populations in pursuit of European manifest destiny in America. (Cooke, 2018, p. 31)

Chapter 14: It's Been a Long Long Time

I am not sure when it happened or how, but it is clear that this piece, like so many of the others, is meant to be performed, not read. I am indeed a performance scholar activist poet, plugging history with current events, contemporary political rhetoric, music, movies, and research. With satire, alliteration, allegory, and rhyme, this piece is meant to be heard. Bob Marley sang, "Emancipate yourselves from mental slavery; none but ourselves can free our minds . . . Won't you help to sing these songs of freedom? 'Cause all I ever have: Redemption songs" (Marley, 1980; see also Parker, 2021). Being Jamaican born inerrantly in that honorific makes me a revolutionary. It is impossible to have Jamaican national heroes like Marcus Garvey (History.com Editors, 2023), Paul Bogle (Day, 2022), Nanny (Gabriel, 2005), and Samuel Sharpe (National Library of Jamaica, 2010) without a spirit of fight and liberation in one's soul—much like "Redemption Song" echoes Marley's words as quoted before his mortal body transitioned from this Earth: "'Redemption Song' have meaning, and I would love to do more like that." Marley added: "I say [in the song] 'Have no fear for atomic energy', because man has hopes. No one can stop the time and you have to live within time, so time is important" (Haider, 2022).

From India Arie (2001; see also Yeo, 2022) to *The Jeffersons* (Malekzadeh, 2012; Nicholl et al., 1975–1985), this piece includes the murders of Black children, such as Trayvon Martin being brutalized in his own neighborhood over a presumed misidentified bag of Skittles, and his murderer still free due to the unjust criminal justice system and the privilege of Whiteness (Buckley, 2013). That a Black woman can call the police for protection and be murdered point blank in front of her child (Bowman, 2023) is something that simply would not happen, and has never happened, to a White woman or person. The presumption of innocence and protection of life is not something extended to Blackness. Even Breonna Taylor (Oppel et al., 2023) was criminalized for being Black and a woman by the simple injustice of nothing being done to avenge her being murdered in her bed in the middle of the night. This poem plays with language, pain, rhetoric, and politics to bring to the forefront images from static to action. As a linguistic scholar, I view even the words we use as an obvious displacement from guilt; *killed* or *death* is much more a statement of fact than the words that should be used—*murdered, attacked, victimized*. These much better fit the situation and action, but will not be used as long as it might shed negative light on the body of Whiteness.

For me, as an African-centered woman who spends time learning to understand the path to the Black situation, learning from scholars who have studied this process, and working to unchain my mind and my thoughts, it is an ever-evolving process. I am much more open to understanding the role Black people play in our own suffering, while recognizing the significant lion's share comes from displacement, location theory implementation, and strategic systematic and structural processes meant to keep the disparities in place. It should also be recognized that there are those who wish to keep it so and those who wish to fight for justice. The difference between co-conspirators and allies, activists, and thought leaders varies widely. I myself now fall under the elitist segment of the populace. Even the title of this poem, running through the entire piece, "It's Been a Long Long Time," is sarcastic. There never seems to be a moment of peace when there is not a tragedy berating the psyche of Black people (Alvarez & Tulino, 2022). Comments like these are common and no longer a shock to the Black community:

> "We're constantly turning on the TV, Facebook, Twitter, Instagram and seeing people that look like us who are getting murdered with no repercussions," said [Carlil] Pittman, an organizer for A New Deal for Youth. "It's not normal to see someone get murdered by the click of a video on your phone, yet it has become the norm for our people, our Black and brown communities." (Stafford, 2021)

The lull between each stanza reinforces the acknowledgment of what's happening, seeing hope through music and movies that are staples among the Black community yet being shocked at every line that these traumas have happened and continue to happen. There is mistrust in the American health system, so Black people are stigmatized for health disparities. There is mistrust among law enforcement, so Black people cry out for "defunding the police" (Fernandez, 2020), but these cries fall on deaf ears, and Black people get labeled for asking too much. There is fear in the education system, because the "school-to-prison pipeline" (Barnes & Motz, 2018) is a setup for the continuation of Jim Crow and free labor (Alexander, 2012). With all the reversal and political demagoguery, it's impossible to imagine the depth of strength that has kept Black people still standing.

> This latest act of terrorism acerbates the cumulative emotional trauma of African Americans. The psychological wound inflicted compounds the legacy of cultural mistrust among the African American community towards specific institutions and symbols. The deeply felt emotional responses to this recent tragedy represents the historical legacy of continuous acts of oppression born out of centuries old beliefs that are linked to an ideology of white supremacy and racism, which all too often are committed as acts of terrorism. (Cooke, 2018, p. 47)

The frustration of loss, the numbness from pain, and the hopelessness of seeing history repeat itself can bring on such a deep sense of devastation that sometimes we just want to forget. Sometimes getting involved in things that are dangerous out of desperation, or as a form of self-medicating, causes overdose (Stevens-Watkins et al., 2012). Sometimes there are suicides to escape the pain. Then there are times when those who feel there is no winning take the position of joining their enemy to survive (White et al., 2014). In the end, this piece speaks to the incredible strength in community, and the power of remembrance. Life always finds a way, and the African spirit will not die.

REFERENCES

Alexander, M. (2012). *The new Jim Crow: Mass incarceration in the age of colorblindness*. The New Press.

Alvarez, A., & Tulino, D. (2022). Racial conflict, violence and trauma: Why race dialogues are critical to healing. *International Journal of Qualitative Studies in Education*, 36(8), 1487–1495.

Arie, I. (2001). Brown skin [Song]. On *Acoustic soul*. Motown Records.

Barnes, J. C., & Motz, R. T. (2018). Reducing racial inequalities in adulthood arrest by reducing inequalities in school discipline: Evidence from the school-to-prison pipeline. *Developmental Psychology*, 54(12), 2328–2340.

Bowman, E. (2023, December 22). *A 27-year-old woman who called 911 for help was fatally shot by an LA deputy*. NPR. https://www.npr.org/2023/12/22/1221113460/la-police-shooting-niani-finlayson-lancaster

Buckley, L. A. (2013, July 13). Zimmerman is acquitted in Trayvon Martin killing. *The New York Times*. https://www.nytimes.com/2013/07/14/us/george-zimmerman-verdict-trayvon-martin.html

Cooke, B. G. (2018). An overview of the impact of racial hate and its manifestation of homegrwon terrorism in America. In P. Hampton-Garland, L. Sechrest-Ehrhardt, & B. G. Cooke (Eds.), *Socio-economic and education factors impacting American political systems* (pp. 29–556). IGI Global.

Day, C. (2022, October 19). *The Morant Bay Rebellion, October 1865*. The National Archives. https://blog.nationalarchives.gov.uk/the-morant-bay-rebellion-october-1865/

DuBois, J. (1980). Movin' on up (Theme from the TV show *The Jeffersons*) [Song]. On *Queen of the Highway*. Som Livre.

Fernandez, P. (2020, June 11). *Defunding the police will actually make us safer*. American Civil Liberties Union. https://www.aclu.org/news/criminal-law-reform/defunding-the-police-will-actually-make-us-safer

Gabriel, D. (2005). *Jamaica's true queen: Nanny of the maroons*. https://jamaicans.com/queennanny/

Haider, A. (2022, July 11). Redemption song: Bob Marley's anthem carries liberating force. *Financial Times*. https://ig.ft.com/life-of-a-song/redemption-song.html

History.com Editors. (2023, December 15). *Marcus Garvey*. History. https://www.history.com/topics/black-history/marcus-garvey

Malekzadeh, S. (2012, August 7). What "The Jeffersons" taught me about being an American. *The Atlantic*. https://www.theatlantic.com/entertain

ment/archive/2012/08/what-the-jeffersons-taught-me-about-being-an-american/260812/

Marley, B. (1980). Redemption song [Song]. On *Uprising*. Island/Tuff Gong.

National Library of Jamaica. (2010). *Samuel "Sam" Sharpe: A forerunner of modern day labour movements*. https://www.nlj.gov.jm/labourday/samsharpe.html

Nicholl, D., Ross, M., & West, B. (Creators). (1975–1985). *The Jeffersons* [TV series]. T.A.T. Communications Company; NRW Productions; Ragamuffin Productions; Embassy Television.

Oppel, R. A., Jr., Taylor, D. B., & Bogel-Burroughs, N. (2023, December 13). What to know about Breonna Taylor's death. *The New York Times*. https://www.nytimes.com/article/breonna-taylor-police.html

Parker, M. (2021, January 24). *Bob Marley "Redemption song" (1980)* [Video]. YouTube. https://www.youtube.com/watch?v=MO9m6PHO_nw

Stafford, K. (2021, April 18). *Black Americans experiencing collective trauma, grief*. WHYY. https://whyy.org/articles/black-americans-experiencing-collective-trauma-grief/

Stevens-Watkins, D., Perry, B., Harp, K. L., & Oser, C. B. (2012). Racism and illicit drug use among African American women: The protective effects of ethnic identity, affirmation, and behavior. *Journal of Black Psychology*, *38*(4), 471–496.

White, I. K., Laird, C. N., & Allen, T. D. (2014, November 20). Selling out? The politics of navigating conflicts between racial group interest and self-interest. *American Political Science Review*, *108*(4), 783–800.

Yeo, A. (2022, February 15). *India Arie explains the bigger problem behind Joe Rogan's racist comments: "I sing about this but I don't really talk about it much."* Mashable. https://mashable.com/video/india-arie-racism-trevor-noah-joe-rogan-spotify

CHAPTER 15
It's the Same Thing

This war against Iraq
Under the false pretense of justice for the Iraqi people
This war
Where people are dying like worthless flies
And their blood brings cries
From mothers of every nation—

It's the same thing

Same as when they brought the Africans here on slave ships
The *Amistad* jam-packed like sardines
And our women disgraced, raped, and no one heard their screams—
Same as the stealing of our precious ivory
And natural resources of Africa's bosom
Using swords and knives and teaching us religion—

It's the same thing
And it goes way farther than that

Goes back to the Spaniards crossing the ocean
Goes back to the Cubans directing those murderers
Who committed mass genocide against the Caribbean

Same as them trying to tell us that Egypt and the river Nile
No longer belonged to Africans
That the people there are the color of snow and not Black like burnt coal in the sand—

It's the same thing

Same as them telling us Black people couldn't be smart enough to build the pyramids
Because the very existence of it still baffles their mediocre minds
Same as them stealing from us under the pretense of civilizing barbarians and industrializing third-world lands
Same as them selling us in shackles
And still they are riding on our back
Selling us crack
Killing us softly with biological warfare that they themselves implemented
And now fear—

It's the same thing

Same as our children's bellies being filled with worms
And our homeless shuffle in empty boxes on the cold concrete floor
Same as them giving us welfare cheese and rewarding us for sitting at home and having babies
And punishing those of us who work hard, follow their laws, and believe in their democracy—

This war
This lie
It's the same thing

And we are not far removed

We are living in slavery and ignorance as this country only tells us what they think we should know

Still shackled by the media who wants to keep our ears glued to blood and gore and not hear the truth

We are still slaves

And the sooner we realize that this war is not about terrorism

The better we will be

The sooner we realize that this war is not about saving the Iraqi people from lives of fear and hate

The better we will be

Because this war is about oil

It's about power

And we are still buying into the crap they feed us—that we are safe—and we go about our everyday lives while they turn and enslave yet another nation

Another group of people just like they did to us

Just like they stole and mutilated the Native American Indians just for their land

This war

It's the same thing

And we are still slaves

Hands and bodies bound by chains and lynched minds

Inside we are still adorned by the patches and leftover fabrics tailored to keep us ignorant

It's the same thing

And we are not that far removed

It's the same thing

And the Iraqi women are still women mourning their loss and crying for peace

It's the same thing
It's the same thing
It's the same thing

March 26, 2003

SCHOLARLY DISCOURSE

It is hard to believe, but in 2024, we can safely say, "It's the same thing!" From the year 2000 to today, there has been war with indirect impact on American life, but most of us are trained to think "out of sight, out of mind." And while we look on in horror, that has not even been the worst of human indignity, as global catastrophes have also ripped at the fabric of the frailty and vulnerability of us all. "Politically, the doctrine of the identity of interests has commonly taken the form of an assumption that every nation has an identical interest in peace, and that any nation which desires to disturb the peace is therefore both irrational and immoral" (Carr, 1946, p. 51). Unfortunately, this ideology has not stopped the onslaught of bloodshed across the globe.

In the past decade, we have witnessed how hatred and racial identity have set us apart in how we think of even the most basic of human needs when we are indoctrinated by disdain for each other based on our skin color. The COVID-19 pandemic left the blame on non-Whites (Neuman, 2020), Haiti and other Caribbean countries were considered "shithole" countries (Fram & Lemire, 2018), and the American government threw toilet paper at Puerto Ricans, saying they are from a different country when they are actually Americans (Silva, 2017). There have been countless genocides in Africa (Prunier, 2011) and Westernization-created coup d'états throughout the Global South (Intercepted, 2022) in order to destabilize and take whatever natural resources are desired, including the people. But that's how it has always been—because people from the Global South were never really thought of as human beings, it was okay to look away, explain it away, or justify away with political rhetoric and misinformed narratives so those who were not impacted could sleep better at night.

However, that has not been the case in the war between Ukraine and Russia. That war has born naked the racist foundational belief of members of the Global North, crying, applauding, and angered that their precious Whiteness (Bayoumi, 2022) is being destroyed, by themselves (Al Jazeera Staff, 2022). There is nowhere to look but at themselves, and no one to blame but themselves, which leaves a gap in their belief system that protects their narrative of elitism and White supremacist thoughts. In the Gaza war, the idea of religion over humanity is the problem that the entire world is having as we look on and watch the genocide against the Palestinians. Everyone agrees that in humanity there is a right to life, liberty, and pursuit of happiness, and everyone deserves this. But to deduce any culture, race, or ethnicity as inhuman (Medet, 2023) in order to eradicate them is wrong.

We need to come to the table more, with honesty, humanity, and historical understanding (BBC, 2023), in order to resolve much of the conflict we are witnessing. But war can be cruel, bloody, and brutal, and the only way to do that is to disassociate oneself from it. "War most often promotes the internal unity of each state involved. The state plagued by internal strife may then, instead of waiting for the accidental attack, seek the war that will bring internal peace" (Waltz, 2001, p. 81). Those standing by are just as guilty as those actively involved. Humanitarians around the world are calling for intervention, but those in power just stand by and watch. As Martin Luther King wrote in his "Letter From Birmingham Jail" on April 16, 1963:

> I must confess that over the past few years I have been gravely disappointed with the white moderate. I have almost reached the regrettable conclusion that the Negro's great stumbling block in his stride toward freedom is not the White Citizen's Councilor or the Ku Klux Klanner, but the white moderate, who is more devoted to "order" than to justice; who prefers a negative peace which is the absence of tension to a positive peace which is the presence of justice; who constantly says: "I agree with you in the goal you seek, but I cannot agree with your methods of direct action"; who paternalistically believes he can set the timetable for another man's freedom; who lives by a mythical concept of time and who constantly advises the Negro to wait for a "more convenient season." Shallow understanding from people of good will is more frustrating than absolute misunderstanding from people of ill will. Lukewarm acceptance is much more bewildering than outright rejection. (American Social History Productions, 2024)

The world sees these crimes and is saddened, disheartened, and afraid. The historical narratives that have been used against one people have been reiterated and ratified as a legitimate and strategic form of extermination. "And now I ask: what else has bourgeois Europe done? It has undermined civilizations, destroyed countries, ruined nationalities, extirpated 'the root of diversity.' No more dikes, no more bulwarks. The hour of the barbarian is at hand. The modern barbarian. The American hour. Violence, excess, waste, mercantilism, bluff, conformism, stupidity, vulgarity, disorder" (Césaire, 1972/2000, p. 76). This is what we now witness, and it's horrific:

Sierra Leone Civil War, 1991–2002
Bosnian War, 1992–1995
Kosovo War, 1998–1999
War in Afghanistan, 2001–2014

Iraq War, 2003–2011
Libya Conflict, 2011–present
Syria Conflict, 2011–present
Yemen Conflict, 2014–present
Global Coalition to Defeat ISIS, 2014–present (Imperial War Museums, 2024; see also Table 15.1)

1990–1991	Persian Gulf War	United States and Coalition Forces vs. Iraq
1995–1996	Intervention in Bosnia and Herzegovina	United States as part of NATO acted as peacekeepers in former Yugoslavia
2001–2021	Invasion of Afghanistan	United States and Coalition Forces vs. the Taliban regime in Afghanistan to fight terrorism
2003–2011	Invasion of Iraq	United States and Coalition Forces vs. Iraq
2004–present	War in Northwest Pakistan	United States vs. Pakistan, mainly drone attacks
2007–present	Somalia and Northeastern Kenya	United States and Coalition forces vs. al-Shabaab militants
2009–2016	Operation Ocean Shield (Indian Ocean)	NATO allies vs. Somali pirates
2011	Intervention in Libya	U.S. and NATO allies vs. Libya
2011–2017	Lord's Resistance Army	U.S. and allies against the Lord's Resistance Army in Uganda
2014–2017	U.S.-led Intervention in Iraq	U.S. and coalition forces against the Islamic State of Iraq and Syria
2014–present	U.S.-led intervention in Syria	U.S. and coalition forces against al-Qaeda, ISIS, and Syria
2015–present	Yemeni Civil War	Saudi-led coalition and U.S., France, and Kingdom against the Houthi rebels, Supreme Political Council in Yemen, and allies
2015–present	U.S. intervention in Libya	U.S. and Libya against ISIS

Table 15.1   Wars With American Involvement Since 1990

Source: From "American Involvement in Wars From Colonial Times to the Present," by M. Kelly, 2020, ThoughtCo (https://www.thoughtco.com/american-involvement-wars-colonial-times-present-4059761).

REFERENCES

Al Jazeera Staff. (2022, February 27). *"Double standards": Western coverage of Ukraine war criticised*. Al Jazeera. https://www.aljazeera.com/news/2022/2/27/western-media-coverage-ukraine-russia-invasion-criticism

American Social History Productions. (2024). *Martin Luther King speaks out against injustice*. Center for Media and Learning, City University of New York. https://shec.ashp.cuny.edu/items/show/684

Bayoumi, M. (2022, March 2). They are "civilised" and "look like us": The racist coverage of Ukraine. *The Guardian*. https://www.theguardian.com/commentisfree/2022/mar/02/civilised-european-look-like-us-racist-coverage-ukraine

BBC. (2023, November 15). *Israel Gaza war: History of the conflict explained*. https://www.bbc.com/news/newsbeat-44124396

Carr, E. H. (1946). *The twenty years' crisis, 1919–1939*. HarperCollins.

Césaire, A. (2000). *Discourse on colonialism* (J. Pinkham, Trans.). Monthly Review Press. (Original work published 1972)

Fram, A., & Lemire, J. (2018, January 11). *Trump: Why allow immigrants from "shithole countries"?* Associated Press. https://apnews.com/article/immigration-north-america-donald-trump-ap-top-news-international-news-fdda2ff0b877416c8ae1c1a77a3cc425

Imperial War Museums. (2024). *Timeline of 20th and 21st century wars*. https://www.iwm.org.uk/history/timeline-of-20th-and-21st-century-wars

Intercepted. (2022, March 9). *U.S.-trained officers have led numerous coups in Africa*. The Intercept. https://theintercept.com/2022/03/09/intercepted-podcast-africa-coup/

Kelly, M. (2020, November 4). *American involvement in wars from colonial times to the present*. ThoughtCo. https://www.thoughtco.com/american-involvement-wars-colonial-times-present-4059761

Medet, H. İ. (2023, October 23). *Israel paints Palestinians as "animals" to legitimize war crimes: Israeli scholar*. Anadolu Agency. https://www.aa.com.tr/en/middle-east/israel-paints-palestinians-as-animals-to-legitimize-war-crimes-israeli-scholar/3030278

Neuman, S. (2020, September 22). *In U.N. speech, Trump blasts China and WHO, blaming them for spread of COVID-19*. NPR. https://www.npr.org/sections/coronavirus-live-updates/2020/09/22/915630892/in-u-n-speech-trump-blasts-china-and-who-blaming-them-for-spread-of-covid-19

Prunier, G. (2011). *Africa's world war: Congo, the Rwandan genocide, and the making of a continental catastrophe*. Oxford University Press.

Silva, D. (2017, October 8). *Trump defends throwing paper towels to hurricane survivors in Puerto Rico*. NBC News. https://www.nbcnews.com/politics/politics-news/trump-defends-throwing-paper-towels-hurricane-survivors-puerto-rico-n808861

Waltz, K. N. (2001). *Man, the state and war: A theoretical analysis*. Columbia University Press.

CHAPTER 16
My Nubian Sisters

My Nubian sisters
Direct descendants from the Egyptian queens of the Nile
You've got to open your eyes
The way we treat our Black men is wrong
Sometimes I wonder if we weren't better off in chains—
Values and morals stood high on our chest
The Black man was strong and humble
Clung to his woman and fought for her with his tears
But today we forget
We forget what it's like to love with our lives
We forget what it's like to die for freedom
But it's remembering that will set us free
The way things are going today
If we don't change
I fear we will find ourselves back in slavery
Bound by shackles we cannot see
Chained and sold into a life we cannot survive
My Nubian sisters
It is in our hands to take hold of our future
To rescue our men and our brothers
To teach knowledge to our sons that no one can devour

We are the answer to our freedom
And in our loins the kings of Alkebulan who will rule forever
Standing strong, me and you
By our men
With their heads cradled in our breast
As we quietly lead
That's the true preface of a love song

October 15, 2015

SCHOLARLY DISCOURSE

Let's talk sisterhood and Black feminism. The great poet and feminist activist Audre Lorde once said, "I am a Black Feminist. I mean I recognize that my power as well as my primary oppressions come as a result of my Blackness as well as my womaness, and therefore my struggles on both of these fronts are inseparable" (quoted in Lewis, 2019). One of the greatest things about humanity is the constant growing, stretching, and shedding we do. At the time this poem, "My Nubian Sisters," was written, I was immersed in Blackness, just stepping onto the pebbled path of interrogating Black history from the lens of Black scholars who have laid out a road map for truth. Black women—and I say Black *women* because the founders of Black Lives Matter (BLM) are women and Black—became activated over Michael Brown's murder in Ferguson, Missouri, and in the summer of 2015, BLM activists refused to be silent when the then demagogue (Asante, 2018) presidential candidate commented that "maybe he should have been roughed up" (Foran, 2015) in regard to an activist protester at a rally. Alicia Garza, Patrisse Cullors, and Opal Tometi are now our warrior sisters, lauding the battle cry of a nation, standing in the gap where Black men are impotent, just like Black women have done historically.

> But today we forget
> We forget what it's like to love with our lives
> We forget what it's like to die for freedom
> But it's remembering that will set us free
> The way things are going today
> If we don't change
> I fear we will find ourselves back in slavery
> Bound by shackles we cannot see
> Chained and sold into a life we cannot survive

Now, within the past decade, I have learned things about the shades of Blackness in the United States that have evolved since 2015—underlying sores that have festered and bubbled up to the surface regarding sisterhood and Blackness, African-ness, Caribbean-ness, and African-American-ness. As a disclaimer, it must be noted that I am not a feminist scholar; I am a political scientist with expertise in Black politics and international relations. My specialization as a linguistic scholar puts me at the intersection of rhetoric narrative and Blackness. Having noted this, I will attempt to denote how other scholars have differentiated between feminist theory, from a Eurocentric lens, and Black feminist theory. This is important to do as, historically, Black bodies have fought a different fight than White bodies, showing that in order for peaceful existence, we must break away from the norm in order to address the needs of the race of specific people. This is why multiple disciplines have a Black society of a similar name: American Political Science Association vs. National Conference of Black Political Scientists; American Sociological Association vs. Association of Black Sociologists; American Psychological Association vs. Association of Black Psychologists; American Medical Association vs. Association of Black Family Medicine Physicians; and so on. It stands to reason, then, that Black feminists would feel ignored in general spaces and need to create more specific spaces to address Black women's particular needs.

> Throughout the nation's history, African American women have struggled with White women on many political fronts. For example, in 1921, at the National Women's Party Convention, Alice Paul received Black delegates' complaints over disenfranchisement with indifference. On another occasion, in 1970, White feminists' reluctance to aggressively organize against the political persecution of Angela Davis continued this legacy of White women rejecting and alienating Black women. These experiences and countless others spurred Black women to have feminist theory and praxis to include issues unique to them. (Taylor, 1998, p. 234)

In a more general definition, according to Amy Allen (1999),

> feminists have an interest in making visible and making sense of the systematic relations of sexist, racist, heterosexist, and class-based denomination and subordination that characterize late capitalist Western pluralist societies. This concern requires an adequate feminist conception of power to shed light on power understood as domination. (p. 2)

My Nubian sisters
It is in our hands to take hold of our future
To rescue our men and our brothers
To teach knowledge to our sons that no one can devour
We are the answer to our freedom

In a fight for freedom, when everyone is hungry, the colonialist psychopathic behavior is to conquer and divide. This is not an attempt *not* to take responsibility for ourselves, our culture, or our existence. In fact, that is all Black people have ever wanted, except the rules to the game always change once we have figured it out. The rhetoric and political assignation of the character of the Black body become amplified, and opportunities become scarce until all one can see is pain and fear. Revisit the discourse discussing the *Willie Lynch Letter* (1990) with the poem "The Broken Bridge" (p. 37). It is written as plain as day. As a matter of point, read the entire book. It is a short, quick read that will get the mind and blood percolating.

It has become palpable that while there was a time—good or bad, right or wrong—when the "one drop" rule (Hollinger, 2005) applied and all women of color were considered Black, African-ness, Caribbean-ness, Latin-American-ness, and African-American-ness were stretched thin when biracialness became a new identity in the census, eradicating that solidarity of Blackness (Blay, 2021). Then all demographics became either White or Afro-something. Africans don't want to be Black or African American (Mwakikagile, 2009), Caribbeans have their own unique identities (Model, 2008), Latin Americans don't want to be associated with Blackness (Olliz-Boyd, 2010), and let's not even begin to discuss the Asian population, also people of color, because the racist connotations toward them may seem positive or their proximity to Whiteness may or may not make them people of color (Kim, 2023). When the racial divide became pulverized with so much more than the very concept of sisterhood, fighting for racial unity, as depicted in "My Nubian Sisters," almost seems null and void. Then colorism—it does not end. But there is more to discuss and more to heal. There is no way to fully explore the notions that have risen around this scholarly discourse. But that's what this is, a conversation that we must all now have in order to heal. As Dr. Crystal Chambers (2023) cited Anna Julia Cooper on the inside front cover of her book, we should remember that "when and where I enter . . . then and there the whole Negro race enters with me."

REFERENCES

Allen, A. (1999). *The power of feminist theory: Domination, resistance, solidarity*. Routledge.

Asante, M. K. (2018). *The American demagogue: Donald Trump in the presidency of the United States of America*. Universal Write Publications.

Blay, Y. (2021, February 22). *How the "one drop rule" became a tool of White supremacy*. Literary Hub. https://lithub.com/how-the-one-drop-rule-became-a-tool-of-white-supremacy/

Chambers, C. (2023). *Black women's pathways to executive academic leadership*. Universal Write Publications.

Foran, C. (2015, December 31). A year of Black Lives Matter. *The Atlantic*. https://www.theatlantic.com/politics/archive/2015/12/black-lives-matter/421839/

Hollinger, D. A. (2005). *One drop and one hate*. Daedalus. https://www.amacad.org/publication/one-drop-one-hate

Kim, C. J. (2023). *Asian Americans in an anti-Black world*. Cambridge University Press.

Lewis, J. J. (2019, January 23). *Audre Lorde quotes*. ThoughtCo. https://www.thoughtco.com/audre-lorde-quotes-3530035

Model, S. (2008). *West Indian immigrants: A Black success story*. Russell Sage Foundation.

Mwakikagile, G. (2009). *Africans and African Americans*. New Africa Press.

Olliz-Boyd, A. (2010). *The Latin American identity and the African diaspora: Ethnogenesis in context*. Cambria Press.

Taylor, U. (1998). The historical evolution of Black feminist theory and praxis. *Journal of Black Studies, 29*(2), 234–253.

The Willie Lynch Letter and The Making of a Slave. (1990). African Tree Press.

CHAPTER 17
Named

Who am I?
I know to whom I am a daughter
And those I should call grandmother
And the spitting image of my father
But when the day is done, I still didn't know where I belonged
So many times I fell and I stumbled
So many times I cried and I fumbled
Not sure who really loved me
Wondering where to find the strength to console myself
Weakened by thoughts of a great spiritual tapestry
Strengthened by word of strangers who saw worth in me
But dislocated
Weathered and worn through the years
Believing there must be more to religion
Questioning the books used for classroom instruction
Filled with righteous indignation
My life was such juxtaposition
Believe and fall in line or keep fighting for a cause I could feel but didn't understand
Intellectually bounded and rooted in the context of my mind
Figment of my imagination
I didn't know what to know

Elders meant well but were lost among the bones that paved the path of the Underground Railroad
A journey living in fire
A rite of passage filled with reckless desires
The rocky road of an unsteady sea
Was the burden of wisdom my ancestors bestowed upon me
And I wondered

Where do I belong?
I know from where I got my first education
From Jamaica I was forced into immigration
From homelessness to starvation
I found the village that rescued me
Afrocentrist without a name—
People with the same cause, same passion yet not the same
My Black hands held by hues of distinct variation—
Black, White, and in between, I am the daughter of every nation
They imparted to me knowledge, told as stories like manna, Black diamonds
The very myth of my being

Without a name I tried to give back
My mentors to make proud I wanted to have an impact
But without a center I was just another lost soul calling out but in the oblivion I sat
I was a wreck, Brown and purposeless
Until the broken road solidified
Memories of them and mine intensified
Academic warfare I was justified

And then . . .
It happened!

With my destiny I collided
Truth and knowledge about self-determination
I learned that my struggle was the beginning of my ascension—
Belief so strong, centered in Alkebulan, in Kemet, and with Egypt, the foundation

Knowledge flowed from the lips of a Great African
Words loosened the blinders from my eyes
I could see the layers, peeled away, and I recognized
The truth finally materialized
Afrocentricity my calling to stand with my ancestors in the fight
An Afrocentrist I am
The revelation is right
A rainbow of justice lightning striking through my core
An anchor in the water of blood I am now permanently clotted
I have endured
I have been found
I now know the reflection I seek
What I didn't know I sought
Ayo Sekai I have been named
And my foundation is the ankh

October 10, 2015

SCHOLARLY DISCOURSE

It's a mantra I echo to anyone who asks that I have always been Afrocentric, even *before* I knew about Afrocentricity. As far back as I can remember, something within me has resonated deeply with my identity. Identities in formative developmental years in children come about through a combination of things. According to Krischa Esquivel and colleagues (n.d.),

> Where we truly start seeing social identities begin is within families and their culture. Where we see social identities cultivated, especially in the classroom is through play. Children develop self-identity, who they believe themselves to be, and begin to form relationships through play and peer relations which contribute to their emotional, social and cognitive development.

They further explain that in the development of personal identity and social identity, cues are taken from

> children's subjective feelings about their distinctiveness from others, their sense of uniqueness, of individuality. Social identity refers, on the other hand, to the ways in which they feel they are (or would like to be) the same as others, typically through identification with family and/or peer culture. (Esquivel et al., n.d.)

It would make sense, then, that in my formative years as a child growing up in the Caribbean, the people, music, and culture imprinted on my sense of identity. Migrating to the United States, as a teenager, I became merged with the new perspective of "Blackness" as it is defined in this country. That Blackness, then, is reflected in those around me, those I respect, my teachers, and the mentors I found in the books I read. In this book, you will find poems going back decades into my early identity and childhood, implying that the nature of my work—resistance pieces, revolutionary mantras, an outcry against political injustices—was the cry of the inner girl who was developing her *asili* (Ani, 1994), though she did not know it yet or even understand what exactly it was . . . which brings me to the paradigm of Afrocentricity.

What is it to be Afrocentric? According to Merriam-Webster (2023), it is "centered on or derived from Africa or the Africans." In my identity development, I grew quite differently in my behavior patterns and character, as discussed in *Yurugu* by Miramba Ani (1994), but it was not until I began my doctoral program at Howard University that I began to learn about Afrocentricity. So, what is Afrocentricity? According to Dr. Molefi Kete Asante (2020), the Father of Afrocentricity,

> Afrocentricity is a philosophical paradigm used to generate theories and methods of analysis and correctives to the social, economic, and cultural conditions of African people. Rather Afrocentricity argued that Africans, regardless to opposition and despite the spatial distribution of Africans, had to embrace the idea that as African people there was nothing wrong with them as Africans. Afrocentricity's innovation in approaching knowledge related to African people is the assertion that Africans must be the center of their own narratives. This was a simple philosophical pivot, but its impact has colored all studies of African people since the publication of [my] original studies on Afrocentricity.

Learning to understand the principles of Afrocentricity was a lightbulb moment for me. I had never heard of Dr. Asante prior to being assigned him as a philosopher in one of my first-year classes, and then I was overwhelmed by how much I didn't know when I googled him. I felt like everything I am, was, or would be was wrapped into this ideology of Afrocentricity my whole life, and I just did not have the words to express it. I suppose I could have just taken the angle to sharing how Dr. Asante named me, and the process, but it has meant so much more to me, being adorned with a name that fits the identity of who I believe myself to be, and that manifested this poem. My evolution and primary years led me to the great scholar and philosopher Dr. Asante, who saw me and gave back to me what was taken away from my ancestors, who were stolen from Africa, placed in concentration camps, and forced into labor. I have been centered, turned right side up to own my identity as a child of Africa, by way of Jamaica, into the United States of America.

REFERENCES

Ani, M. (1994). *Yurugu: An African-centered critique of European cultural thought and behavior.* Afrikan World Books.

Asante, M. K. (2020). Afrocentricity. In R. Rabaka (Ed.), *Routledge handbook of pan-Africanism* (pp. 147–158). Taylor & Francis Group. https://www.taylorfrancis.com/chapters/edit/10.4324/9780429020193-10/afrocentricity-molefi-kete-asante

Esquivel, K, Elam, E., Paris, J., & Tafoya, M. (n.d.). *How children develop identity.* LibreTexts: Social Sciences. https://socialsci.libretexts.org/Bookshelves/Early_Childhood_Education/The_Role_of_Equity_and_Diversity_in_Early_Childhood_Education_(Esquivel_Elam_Paris_and_Tafoya)/03%3A_The_Development_of_Identity_in_Children/3.02%3A_How_Children_Develop_Identity

Merriam-Webster. (2023). *Afrocentric.* https://www.merriam-webster.com/dictionary/Afrocentric

CHAPTER 18
Namesake Alone

Being Jamaican is more than a birthright
Being Jamaican also means to be Black
The many faces of darkness we see
Running around the island
Are only mirrors to reflect the true image of the natives

We vary in color, shape, and size
And exude the beautiful mysteries of the universe
We are strong, proud, and unshaken
In our demeanor to a point of arrogance

Being Jamaican and Black
We stake our claim to our land and our birthright

It is our home.

We cannot hide behind color or strange-sounding surnames
We cannot run during times of controversy
We must stay to stake our claim
We cannot say our father is from here, and our mother from there
Because we are a country of many
But in our veins flows one blood . . .

It is not being raised in a country that makes you a countryman
Or learning to speak our patois
It's knowing and surviving our struggles and hardships
And rejoicing when we overcome
It's sharecropping and sharing
It's dying and being born
It's knowing the rhythm of our music
Through which
We praise
Give thanks
Hate
And warn
It's knowing that blood was spilled there
To give me a right to be here
It's knowing the names of our ancestors
Who died without a care
For me
Whose face they've never seen

When I am hungry
It is they who remind me
I have hands and fertile land
And with time and love it will feed me

So don't tell me you're Jamaican
For Jamaican namesake alone
Show me your island battle scars
That give you the right
To call my island your home!!!

December 30, 1997

SCHOLARLY DISCOURSE

After the assimilation period of rhyming verse, the beat of the poetic drum bursts into the scene. Poetry of revolt, but which is also analytical and descriptive. The poet must, however, understand that nothing can

Chapter 18: Namesake Alone

replace the rational and irreversible commitment on the side of the people in arms.

—Frantz Fenon, *The Wretched of the Earth* (2004, p. 162)

The "poetry of revolt," brought to life, weaves resistance like threads of DNA into the communication style of the African diaspora. Like most Caribbean people, Jamaicans have a very strong heritage, grounded in culture and pride. This is not unlike Global Africa, where food, music, geography, and ancestry fuel the blood of revolutionaries. Language is a big part of this culture (see Figure 18.1). Patois is blended into everything that makes a Jamaican *yaadie*. As colonialism and imperialistic nations have long forged upon the African diaspora, co-opting and foraging everything in their wake, there has been a concerted effort of resistance that remains unshakeable, and that is how language is used to protect, guide, and uplift.

In Jamaica, the language is deeply rooted in music, especially revolution songs. The music, much like this poem, was meant to teach, and uplift pride and ownership in culture. "Bob Marley told people not to be ashamed of their roots; and the Wailers continuously wailed about the conditions of their neighborhood—Trenchtown—while admonishing the

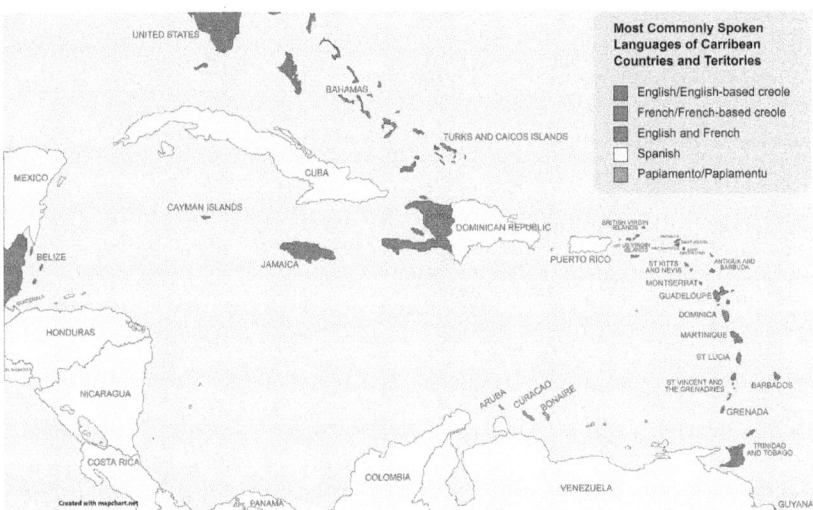

Figure 18.1 Map of the Caribbean Showing the Main Languages Spoken

Source: "Most Commonly Spoken Languages of Caribbean Countries and Territories," by northbynortheast31, 2021, r/MapPorn (https://www.reddit.com/r/MapPorn/comments/mridzu/most_commonly_spoken_languages_of_caribbean/).

youths not to be drawn into the competitiveness and viciousness of the society" (Campbell, 1987, p. 135). In the spirit of poetic expression now infused as poetical science, the famous Louise Bennett must be invoked in looking at how language infuses a culture:

> She was described as Jamaica's leading comedienne, as the "only poet who has really hit the truth about her society through its own language," and as an important contributor to her country of "valid social documents reflecting the way Jamaicans think and feel and live." Through her poems in Jamaican patois, she raised the dialect of the Jamaican folk to an art level which is acceptable to and appreciated by all in Jamaica. In her poems she was able to capture all the spontaneity of the expression of Jamaicans' joys and sorrows, their ready, poignant and even wicked wit, their religion and their philosophy of life. Her first dialect poem was written when she was fourteen years old. (Jamaica Information Service, 2024)

Bennett's passion for the Jamaican language is incomparable. Along with Oliver Samuels (Jamaicans.com, 2020) and the Brother Anansi (About Jamaica, 2016), Jamaican stories have riveted the essence of Jamaicans and helped them to settle into a unshakable identity. Bro' Anansi, the troublemaker, the mischievous spider, not only taught us how to be cunning amid the amount of trouble he got into, but also gave us wise, gnarly, creative ways to get out of said trouble. All of this culminates in the strength of the Jamaican culture and language, which brings a unique insight on life and into the lived experiences of every man, woman, and child from Jamaica. Patois not only identifies one as Jamaican, but the depth of experience, the level of cultural connectivity, and, sometimes, how one shows up, communicates, and conducts business are steeped into how the community is defined, determined, and examined by fellow Jamaicans.

> The strength and influence of the Jamaican language (Jamiekan langwij) system are easily discerned by the fact that during slavery, in post-slavery society, through the nineteenth and twentieth centuries, into the twenty-first century, Jamaican Creole/Patwa has remained one of the main cultural products of the society. Born out of the contact among West/Central African cultural and language groups and European languages (primarily English), the Jamaican language (Jamiekan langwij) that was created was/is functional, colourful, dynamic and was/is an important symbol of "creolity." Armed with the power of that language, Jamaicans, enslaved and free, during slavery and after its demise, continue/d to add new layers of complexity to their "nation language," to their Jamiekan langwij. In a rendering of Lillian Allen's observation in "Language," one of her poems in her "Tribute to Miss Lou," the Jamiekan people have made it clear that "the langwij of the people is the langwij of life." (Johnson, 2023, p. 111)

However, as this poem speaks of pride, culture, and struggle, these attributes are not unique to Jamaica. They are part and parcel of Africans wherever you may find them—symptoms of an ailment called colonialism forced upon the bodies of those still amplifying the strength of the cradle of civilization. The fact is that language will always be part of a revolution, the stronghold of identity, and the foundation of the spirit of a people. As a matter of fact,

> Language is the quintessential ingredient of culture. In the antbellum South, White America understood all too well the consequences of succumbing to the Black quest for literacy, and thus Blacks were not permitted to learn to read and write English. White fears were so great that they even forbade Blacks from developing a distinct form of verbal expression. (Green & Smart, 1997, p. 521)

This amplification of language, a structural means of communication, was always set in the roots of survival. Not having the oppressor understand the communication is key to revolutionary processes. This is the plight and power of the downtrodden, where oppressed people are found throughout the world.

It is Global Africa, which includes Black Africans in America, Europe, Latin America, and the Caribbean. Across all diasporas, language is a unique aspect of the people, giving them sovereignty among themselves, creating saliency toward being free. In this movement toward finding freedom in captivity, Rosier (2020) describes living, breathing societies, where groups create structures of independence while being dependent on one another: "Black people reside within the United States as its nation, with language, culture, economic ideologies, beliefs, and religious structures" (p. 130). Within this stronghold, there is a duality of sovereignty. It makes sense, then, that creoles and multiple forms of language creation manifested out of the need for survival, building community among the marginalized groups, and strengthening the ability to self-regulate and self-identify. Some cultures consider the formation of languages, which is a blend of multiple languages, creole. Creole is explored more deeply in the text *Contact Languages*, in which Bartens (2013) discusses Indigenous Maroons, from countries such as "Guyana, especially present-day Suriname, the mountainous regions of Jamaica—formed settlements based on common ethnic origins" (p. 67), and further elaborates on creole states, such as Palmares, Suriname, Palenque de San Basilio, Colombia, and Venezuela, where many Indigenous groups still practice and rely heavily on a trusted language source. Interestingly, what is generally termed *creole* has a variation of names within those language structures identified by the people who use it. Parkvall and Bakker (2013) named this linguistic terminology *pidgin*, which exists in Jamaica and is used among children, along with creole.

Two very distinguished forms of creole, Gullah Geechee and Ebonics, that are very steeped in culture, resistance, and reclamation of identity, however, are either misunderstood or under attack. There is a major contention that has manifested as a competition between Caribbean Americans, African Americans, and African immigrants to America—an intercultural conversation about who has culture, who is better, and whose fight should be stronger. At the end of this discussion that has no real conclusion or, better yet, is not to be concluded, there is no such answer to be attained; nor are there rewards to be had, as all people who are phenotypically Black, through the social contrast of race and the "racial contract" (Mills, 1997), fall inside the nation-state of Black oppression, struggling for sovereignty in someone else's home (Rosier, 2020). So as "not to put words in anybody's mouth," this discussion bubbles up where some say that African Americans have no real culture, or are not rooted, because they were born in America, direct descendants of those who were brought here across the Atlantic. Those in the Caribbean, in contrast, have carved out their own identity and are separated from their colonial "master" on their own land, while Africans get to live and grow on the African continent and have a unique identifier as the spirit of the people of origin. Despite it all, somehow, they all land in the Global North in search of something lost, like children given up at birth who find love in an adoptive family yet search their whole lives to find the ones who have abandoned, forgotten, or abused them. Though the United States did not give birth to Blackness, as all people have the same origin in Africa, the United States has participated extensively and, in many cases, brutally in the abuse of Black people despite what part of the world they repatriate from. And this is where approval is sought by all; approval of identity, a fight for agency, and language and culture become the battleground. In this fight is the power of resistance and resilience. The pushback is relentless in its later-focused desire that will not be denied. In the American South rises one of the most fascinating resistance languages, the Gullah of the Geechee people, noted as

> the locus classicus for the study of "African survivals" in North American culture. As such, they have been saddled with the duty to generate universal principles for the explanation of Africans' acculturation, adaptation, and cultural resistance in the western hemisphere. (Matory, 2008, p. 949)

For that very reason, such languages should remain sheltered and protected from those who constantly seek to disrupt, co-opt, or destroy. Like Blackness, the culture and languages of marginalized peoples—the largest demographic of people in the world living oppressed—there is an energy to it all, a sense of being and spirit that one cannot experience unless they have lived it. As Miles (2023) tells us,

> To find the South is to locate the experiences, noises, silences, movements, feelings, and memories that make something that we call South possible.

It requires paying attention to the softest and hardest parts of people whose insides hold the South even when the physical body isn't there. It requires being still, dancing, listening, yelling, and being in the South. You have to vibe with the South to get a glimpse of where it is. (p. xii)

Ebonics, or Black English, has been treated as the bastard of language. Children are ridiculed and admonished to "talk right" or accused of lack of intelligence when overheard. However, the more contempt it receives, the more it is rooted as a language of resistance, cultural heritage, and pride, and we see it show up in music, comedy, hairstyles, and even the look and feel of Ebonics when it is co-opted by non-Black people. This is one way that raciolinguistics manifests itself, when non–persons of color use language to construct not just *what* race is but *who* it is, what it looks like, and how people should feel about it. However, it should be clear that "Ebonics, a blend of *ebony* and *phonics*, is a racially affirmative term that was first coined in the Black pride era to refer to the full communicative competence of African-American slave descendants" (Ronkin & Karn, 1999, p. 361). It is not surprising that something that evolved out of survival and resistance would be demonized, though there is not much people of color have to do to fall within the clutches of inferiority in their imperialistic host nation. One just needs to be, well, anything other than White. This is why the concepts of glottopolitics (Phillipson, 1990) and raciolinguistics (Flores & Rosa, 2023) are at an intersection of the racial contract (Mills, 1997) and linguistic imperialism (Phillipson, 1992). Despite Ebonics being demonized as ghetto, bad grammar, and slang, "In December 1996, the Oakland California School Board passed a resolution acknowledging the existence and legitimacy of Ebonics and proposed to use this nonstandard variety of English as a strategy for teaching Standard American English" (Seymour et al., 1999, p. 66). Essentially, what this law does is what it means to fully bring representation to the forefront. If a child sees themselves as visible, then that child can learn.

Understanding how language intersects with culture is critical to the learning modules, frameworks for success, and theories in nation-state development. Ignoring the implications of the historical linguicide, linguistic imperialism, and racioliguistics in framing a nation that is already indebted to humanity is setting a path to international cultural identity suicide.

REFERENCES

About Jamaica. (2016, November 9). *Anansi the spider: What's behind the name!* https://www.about-jamaica.com/anansi_the_spider/

Bartens, A. (2013). Creole languages. In P. Bakker & Y. Matras (Eds.), *Contact languages: A comprehensive guide* (pp. 65–158). Walter de Gruyter.

Campbell, H. (1987). *Rasta and resistance: From Marcus Garvey to Walter Rodney*. Africa World Press.

Fenon, F. (2004). *The wretched of the earth* (R. Philcox, Trans.). Grove Press.

Flores, N., & Rosa, J. (2023). Undoing raciolinguistics. *Journal of Raciolinguistics*, 27(5), 421–427.

Green, C., & Smart, I. I. (1997). Ebonics as cultural resistance. *Peace Review*, 9(4), 521–526.

Jamaica Information Service. (2024). *Famous Jamaicans: Louise Bennett-Coverley*. https://jis.gov.jm/information/famous-jamaicans/louise-bennett-coverley/

Jamaicans.com. (2020). *Oliver Samuels: The Jamaican king of comedy*. https://jamaicans.com/oliver-samuels-the-jamaican-king-of-comedy/

Johnson, M. A. (2023). "Saying dis, dat, and toder": Creating a Jamaican language (Jamiekan langwij) in the eighteenth and nineteenth centuries. In M. A. Johnson (Ed.), *Louise Bennett and Jamiekan langwij: Commemorations and critical perspectives* (pp. 93–119). Africa World Press.

Matory, J. L. (2008). The illusion of isolation: The Gullah/Geechees and the political economy of African culture in the Americas. *Comparative Studies in Society and History*, 50(4), 949–980.

Miles, C. J. (2023). *Vibe: The sound and feeling of Black life in the American South*. University Press of Mississippi.

Mills, C. W. (1997). *The racial contract*. Cornell University Press.

northbynortheast31. (2021). *Most commonly spoken languages of Caribbean countries and territories*. r/MapPorn. https://www.reddit.com/r/MapPorn/comments/mridzu/most_commonly_spoken_languages_of_carribean/

Parkvall, M., & Bakker, P. (2013). Pidgins. In P. Bakker & Y. Matras (Eds.), *Contact lanuages: A comprehensive guide* (pp. 15–64). Walter de Gruyter.

Phillipson, R. (1990). Glottopolitics and linguistic warfare. *World Englishes*, 9(1), 85–94.

Phillipson, R. (1992). *Linguistic imperialism*. Oxford University Press.

Ronkin, M., & Karn, H. E. (1999). Mock Ebonics: Linguistic racism in parodies of Ebonics on the internet. *Journal of Sociolinguistics*, 3(3), 360–382.

Rosier, D. (2020). *Linguistic imperialism: An analysis of the political rhetoric of domination against and through the African American lens* (28315288) [Doctoral dissertation, Howard University]. ProQuest. https://www.proquest.com/openview/129cf6377df913514130e1d51fed3906/1?pq-origsite=gscholar&cbl=18750&diss=y

Seymour, H. N., Abdulkarim, L. M., & Johnson, V. M. (1999). The Ebonics controversy: An educational and clinical dilemma. *Topics in Language Disorders*, 19(4), 66–77.

CHAPTER 19
Oblivion

I don't know what will happen
The outcome
The sensation sylphlike and free
Unknowing
Drifting like a water log along life's path
Bumping against ragged banks of ruptured water
Falling downstream as salmon swim up

I am lost
Taken away by gravity
Trying to live in insanity but reality has taken over
Society says
Nature does
I am caught between two
Not living
No longer present I am being washed, stroked, caressed
Spiritually confused
Don't want to be here
But embraced by the oneness of existence
I float

Lying still in mid-universe
My mind wanders
My feet lithe as feathers
Nimble
Agile
I fly
Blowing kisses to nature's anger
I repent
Falling into fragments of molecules dissolving
Melting into warmth
Cuddled as textured pieces of pores expand and separate
The un-creation of the created
Drifting
Taken
No longer present
Gone

December 10, 2009

SCHOLARLY DISCOURSE

Mental health and healing are the theme of this piece. Though each is left to the interpretation of the reader, the scholarly discourse is meant to tease the possibilities. As poetry is interpretative by those who read it, this is not an attempt to change the inference on the piece as much as it is to add context to some of my sociopolitical, cultural, and demographic influences at the time this piece was written. As a Black-centered woman, I was deeply impacted by the media, politics, and social events. In 2009, the United States was still crippled by one of the largest financial crashes (Soros, 2009) when the economic bubble popped and millions of people lost their security and livelihood, declared bankruptcy, and were starting over. With this came an uncertainty, confusion, and lack of safety among Americans. "According to the U.S. Department of Health and Human Services (HHS) National Center for Health Statistics (NCHS), suicide was the 10th leading cause of death in the United States" (Piscopo, 2017) in 2009, and the National Survey on Drug Use and Health (NSDUH) recorded the highest suicide rates between 18- and 25-year-olds. Those numbers were even more striking among BIPOC individuals, taking into consideration "the legacy of race, inequality and stratification may have provided incentives for financial institutions to engage in racially predatory lending practices that increased the level of risk—which ultimately caused the collapse of the subprime mortgage market, and the attendant financial crisis" (Price, 2010, p. 231). There were always discrepancies in the racial wealth gap in the United States when it comes to inequity in households of color, and according to "2001 to 2013 data from the Survey of Consumer Finances, we show that after peaking in 2007, racial inequalities for most debt types returned to prefinancial crisis levels" (Seamster & Charron-Chénier, 2017, p. 199).

The levels of racial undertones toward Black America were beginning to seep through the frays of hate and fear as Americans looked toward a new presidential candidate who would save them. As citizens took to the voting box, a relative unknown called Barack Obama shocked the nation, bringing a sweeping message of hope, and in retrospect, after two terms of his presidency and two U.S. presidents since he left office, the debate is still not about his policies but about his race (Asante, 2016, p. 61). This discussion serves to say that morale was low in the United States, and that the strain and hardship even hit immigrants (Tesfai, 2017) is another level of discussion for a later date. It stands to reason that there may be some correlation between the downward spiral of mental health in 2008 (McInerney et al., 2013) and today's suffering after another powerful wipeout of hundreds of thousands of people with preexisting conditions and health issues in the COVID-19 pandemic (Beckman, 2020). In 2024, the world is more aware of mental health than ever before. The elite bubble has popped between rich and poor, privileged and disadvantaged, on the tails of famous athletes speaking up about mental health (University of Utah Health, 2017) and abuse (Long et al., 2023), as well as actors and actresses stepping down from the pedestal to show their humanity (Kaul & Chaudhri, 2017). The equalizer of death and illness, fear and pain, has closed the gap of privilege, and even as those things are the best of being human, it has exposed vulnerabilities that have left those in power to enact a level of vengeance and rage on the marginalized in the only way they know how—a psychopathic way, attempting to secure the survival of who they are, their identity, and what it means for reality through their lens.

> The psychological impact of sustaining and exhibiting generations of hate, prejudice, bias and bigotry increases unsubstantiated suspicions, anxieties and fears about the cultured productivity of all members of the human family. Left unchecked, interpersonal hatred turned outward against others as anger or rage destroys the constitutional right to life of others; increases the resentment of another's humanity; and can lead to the objectification and annihilation of another's existence. (Cooke, 2018, p. 50)

Within the context of this piece of work, oxymorons and contradictions rise and fall on waves of emotional expression. I hope it is able to give a sense of being and belonging in retrospect. The commonality in our humanity is the foundational fabric of hope and the survival spirit of mankind.

REFERENCES

Asante, M. K. (2016). *Lynching Barak Obama: How Whites tried to string up the president*. Universal Write Publications.

Beckman, B. P. (2020). *COVID-19: Never seen anything like this ever!* National Library of Medicine.

Cooke, B. G. (2017). An overview of the impact of racial hate and its manifestation of homegrown terrorism in America. In P. Hampton Garland, L. Sechrest-Ehrhardt, & B. G. Cooke (Eds.), *Socio-economic and education factors impacting American political systems: Emerging research and opportunities* (pp. 29–56). Information Science Reference.

Kaul, A., & Chaudhri, V. (2017). Do celebrities have it all? Context collapse and the networked publics. *Journal of Human Values*, 24(1), 1–10. https://doi.org/10.1177/0971685817733568

Long, S., Gelhoren, G., & Clancy, M. (2023, May 5). *27 celebrities who have bravely opened up about being sexually assaulted*. SheKnows. https://www.sheknows.com/entertainment/slideshow/5839/celebs-whove-spoken-out-about-being-sexually-assaulted/

McInerney, M., Mellor, J. M., & Hersch Nicholas, L. (2013). Recession depression: Mental health effects of the 2008 stock market crash. *Journal of Health Economics*, 32(6), 1090–1104.

Piscopo, K. D. (2017, September 27). *Suicidality and death by suicide among middle-aged adults in the United States*. Substance Abuse and Mental Health Services Administration. https://www.samhsa.gov/data/sites/default/files/report_3370/ShortReport-3370.html

Price, G. N. (2010). The subprime crisis and African Americans—Response. *The Review of Black Political Economy*, 37(3–4), 231–236. https://journals.sagepub.com/doi/10.1007/s12114-010-9076-9?icid=int.sj-full-text.similar-articles.2

Seamster, L., & Charron-Chénier, R. (2017). Predatory inclusion and education debt: Rethinking the racial wealth gap. *Social Currents*, 43(3), 199–207. https://iro.uiowa.edu/esploro/outputs/9984196442802771

Soros, G. (2009). *The crash of 2008 and what it means: The new paradigm for financial markets*. Public Affairs.

Tesfai, R. (2017). Continued success or caught in the housing bubble? Black immigrants and the housing market crash. *Population Research and Policy Review*, 36, 531–60. https://link.springer.com/article/10.1007/s11113-017-9429-1

University of Utah Health. (2017, April 26). *10 celebrities who struggle with mental health*. https://healthcare.utah.edu/healthfeed/2017/04/10-celebrities-who-struggle-mental-health

CHAPTER 20
A People Dying

I look around at my people
And feel a profound sense of sadness
My beautiful sistahs
With Samson locks flowing over their shoulders
That already bear the weight of the world
My girlfriends struggling
Trying to make a difference . . .
My mother!

I look around and see what we have been reduced to—
Minds so brilliant, we cascade across Ethiopian legacy
But so poor is this country our chains scrape across the ground—
Mingling with the dog shit and piss
Caretakers to the White man's children
As our own go un-nurtured
Lacking attention and love
While they figure out more ways at their precious desk jobs
To destroy our ancestry

I am deeply pensive and growing increasingly perplexed
At what fate awaits me
My family
My village
My legacy

October 7, 2004

SCHOLARLY DISCOURSE

Why global warming rears its ugly head on the ingestion of this piece can be debated. However, the fear and concern for the future is very real. Concerns about our humanity are only as relative as humans exist, and every parent is concerned about the world that they will leave behind for their children. The daily fights over food insecurity (Long et al., 2005), justice and equity (Carley & Konisky, 2020), racial impartiality (Bright, 2008), globalization (Drache, 1999), and education all lead to the hope that once all the fighting is finished, there will be something left to live for.

If we focus on the one reason for living that human beings have in common, that is this piece of rock called Earth that we all occupy, but

> historical record and observations of other variable stars and the analysis of the relationship between the length of the sunspot cycle and global surface temperatures indicate that pronounced fluctuation in the solar output may occur. For the sake of argument, let us reject such a possibility in the foreseeable future, and assume, on the contrary, that the climate's temperature is controlled, among other factors, by sulfate aerosols emitted into the atmosphere by man-made industry and naturally occurring volcanoes. Even then, if humans keep putting invisible pollutants into the atmosphere at the present rate, "unnatural" greenhouse warming could itself become important soon; its signature must eventually break through the temperature record if it has not already done so, making the terrestrial weather system quite energetic. Thus, uncertainties in future forecast of global warming are great, a significant overall warming of the atmosphere, the surface and the bottom of earth masses (like permafrost under mountains) due to anthropogenic emissions of greenhouse gases ought to occur sometime in this century. In the global climate record, the period 1979–97 is one of the periods of greatest warming during the past 150 years and is the warmest period on record. A four-year study recently completed by ICSI (International Commission on Snow and Ice) predicts that all the glaciers in the central and eastern Himalayas could disappear by the year 2035 due to global warming. (Ansari, 2007, p. 191)

Seems easy enough, but the rich get richer (Mantel, 1995) and have plans to get more so in order to buy their own rocket ships and make their way to the next "Mars" nirvana (Fernholz, 2018). The poor and marginalized will still be in the same place, left to suffer and die. Maybe those who survive the next ice age must be those in power. Or will it be those who have the most power? Or those who are famous? As you dissect this piece, include this in your research:

> I am deeply pensive and growing increasingly perplexed
> At what fate awaits me
> My family
> My village
> My legacy

This is the real concern, because without life, legacy, and something worth dying for, will there even be a history to live to tell these stories about?

REFERENCES

Ansari, M. A. (2007). Statistical aspects of global warming. *Arabian Journal for Science and Engineering, 30*(2A), 189–201.

Bright, S. B. (2008). The failure to achieve fairness: Race and poverty continue to influence who dies. *University of Pennsylvania Journal of Constitutional Law, 11*(1). https://papers.ssrn.com/sol3/papers.cfm?abstract_id=2767916

Carley, S., & Konisky, D. M. (2020). The justice and equity implications of the clean energy transition. *Nature Energy, 5,* pp. 569–577.

Drache, D. (1999, February). *Globalization: Is there anything to fear?* CSGR Working Paper No. 23/99. https://papers.ssrn.com/sol3/papers.cfm?abstract_id=153089

Fernholz, T. (2018). *Rocket billionaires: Elon Musk, Jeff Bezos, and the new space race.* Mariner Books.

Long, S. P., Ainsworth, E. A., Leakey, A. D. B., & Morgan, P. B. (2005). Global food insecurity: Treatment of major food crops with elevated carbon dioxide or ozone under large-scale fully open-air conditions suggests recent models may have overestimated future yields. *Philosophical Transactions of the Royal Society B, 360*(1463), 2011–2020.

Mantel, R. R. (1995). Why the rich get richer and the poor get pooer. *Ciclo de Seminarios, 95*(4), 1–33.

CHAPTER 21
Pride and Prejudice

Before God and all Mankind, we must erase the hate

WHITE MASK
I may look White, but my heart is good
It is from my history that I am misunderstood
The KKK is not the blood that stirs my veins
My tears of regret cannot heal your pain
Look at me, don't judge me by my shade
If we join together, a better history can be made

BLACK MASK
Looking Black does not make me less
I too have suffered and survived the test
Slavery is a legacy hanging over my head
We must now learn from those who are dead
Hatred and prejudice must now be placed in the ground
Wash the blood from our hands and lay our crosses down

MASK WITH NO EYES

Being blind does not mean I can't see
I'm still flesh and blood
Touch me! You'll see I'm real
Those who despise me are handicapped by lies
My eyes may be closed but my heart does not disguise

MASK WITH A SWASTIKA

I too struggled and suffered from pain
Being Jewish, I was nailed to the cross
My people's pain cannot be taken away
But in my mind I grow stronger every day
Love is the healer, we must now begin
To heal the wounds from Hitler's sin

MASK TURNED INSIDE OUT

Being gay, crippled, green, pink, or blue
You'll find a way to hate me too
I did not choose what I would be
But I am in control of the person you now see
I am only human, I can't do it by myself
I am overwhelmed by society's selfishness
You force me in a corner, then when I react
My diversity becomes a target for you to attack
Racism and prejudice is simply wrong
Our rainbow of differences should help make us strong
Love is a bridge broken by neglect
To continue to hate
Continues the cycle of pain and regret

October 30, 1996

SCHOLARLY DISCOURSE

First they came for the socialists, and I did not speak out—because I was not a socialist.

Then they came for the trade unionists, and I did not speak out—because I was not a trade unionist.

Then they came for the Jews, and I did not speak out—because I was not a Jew.

Then they came for me—and there was no one left to speak for me.

—Martin Niemöller (U.S. Holocaust Memorial Museum, 2023)

From wars to social movements, there are those who speak out, march, and take a stand. Sometimes to their detriment. There is so much to fight for when it comes to society, prejudice, racism, discrimination, and marginalization, and there is always a moral question at play. Who am I? What's my position? What do I believe? Whom do I trust, believe, and agree with? Much like sport, there is someone who wins and someone who loses, and even in that, there is so much pain on both sides. The posing question here, though, is does there have to be a winner and a loser? Is it possible to have compromises of give and take, much like a relationship? Sometimes one gets the lion's share of the dispute, and sometimes less so, but both leave one satiated, knowing that there is a care and fairness to look forward to at all times. The quote from Martin Niemöller is important here. His is the story of a man, much like many of us, living through a turning point in history, where everyone must make a moral judgment and decide where they stand. In Niemöller's case, he was a pastor who did not think that the radical Nazi ideas were that bad (U.S. Holocaust Memorial Museum, 2023). There is a moral karma that has been told and retold in movies, stories, and media, of people who did not help the weak, and so they themselves became victimized.

This applies even outside of a major political event. What if it was a child being bullied in school? Abuse or rape? A hit and run, or something as small as returning something valuable that was lost? There comes a time that everyone must ask themselves, "When do we step in?" When is it not okay to stand on the sidelines or stick our heads in the sand? In the past ten years alone, the United States has endured major movements that signified turning points in history, depicting what direction the country will go in. Many of these are due to poverty, food deserts, child welfare, women's rights, and racial issues all standing on the pinnacle of change, and many can remember not just where they were when these events occurred but where they stood within their humanity. Were you an ally or an adversary, and what travesty were you culpable to, because you did nothing but stand by and watch?

Here's one that you might remember. Many can place themselves at this moment in time, remembering how they felt, reacted, and thought about the event. Not as heavy but just as impactful as Black Lives Matter, that is, was the fight to increase the federal minimum wage from $7.25 in 2021 to $15 by 2025. What's the big deal, right? Well, this increase was very necessary because multiple individuals working in the food service industry were barely surviving. Most people were not tipping or at least not tipping well, and the need to discuss and address the food service class was beginning to weigh on the country's conscience. Many wondered what the fight was about and did not get involved. They just figured "whatever happens happens" and they'll go along with it. But this small thing—raising the minimum wage to match rising food costs, interest rates, clothing prices, and inflation, especially depending on where one lives—was a major political agenda for anyone wishing to hold office. This was so big that it drove a larger wedge between the two dominating political parties, causing "divisions among Democrats . . . , pitting liberal lawmakers against their more centrist colleagues and highlighting fissures that have emerged in Democratic strongholds elsewhere, particularly in areas with some of the country's highest costs of living" (Niedzwaidek, 2023). It took years to finally pass, but

> [t]he Raise the Wage Act of 2021, introduced in the U.S. House of Representatives on January 26, 2021, would gradually raise the federal minimum wage to $15 an hour by 2025. EPI [Economic Policy Institute] research shows that raising the federal minimum wage to $15 an hour by 2025 would lift pay for 32 million workers across the country—that's 21% of the U.S. workforce. The increases would provide an additional $107 billion in wages for the country's lowest-paid workers, with the average affected worker who works year-round receiving an extra $3,300 a year. (Multimedia, 2021)

Why was this such a difficult thing to do, when so many across the United States are living in less-than-ideal conditions? Billions of dollars go to U.S. defense every year when the American people are starving. The justification is typically the same narrative, and as recently as last year, the argument was made to "counter growing inflation and rising security threats, prompting lawmakers to increase the fiscal year 2023 defense authorization by $45 billion over Biden's $813 billion request" (Bugos, 2023). All this continues, even when, in any city, along the outskirts are littered bodies of the living, huddled in trash for warmth when it is cold, and eating from that same trash for nourishment. It is easier to pretend that it is "them" and not "us" when, in reality, many of us are living from paycheck to paycheck.

The Black Lives Matter movement gave the United States an opportunity to accept responsibility for the injustices levied against one group of people, but failed. One book noted that there are "two Black societies, separate and unequal" (Taylor, 2016, p. 6), using President Obama as a sign of opulence while Black people in general struggle. It's a form of gaslighting when a large majority of underrepresented groups are struggling and the rest of the world is pointing to a choice few who don success to counter the cries for help and stifle resistance. But what was the mission of Black Lives Matter, and where did everyday citizens stand by the wayside? The name alone is

> meant to be transformative of a nation and its citizens who benefit regularly from white privilege and/or practice or embrace or passively accept white supremacy. But "black lives matter" is also an inflection point for black Americans, a way of dealing with the age-old problem of figuring out what it means to be black and brown in America. (Lebron, 2023, p. xvii)

This movement was equally accepted by those it proposed to protect and rejected by those who have stood against Black equity for centuries. Though we can discuss the many atrocities that surrounded this movement, it is important to show that in the heat of adversity, humanity came through. The protesters did not stand by and let a counterprotester die during the onset of the Black Lives Matter movement, where there was lots of contention among protesters and counterprotesters, each standing for what they thought was right. But in the midst, something extraordinary happened. Black protesters on the side of Black Lives Matter rushed in to protect a White man, a counterprotester who was against the movement and got caught in the fray (Bloomberg Quicktake, 2020). Heroes of humanity rose to this man's defense, refusing to watch someone, who had as much right as they did, get hurt. Yet, how many stood by and watched police violate the rights of Black Lives Matter members during the march protesting the murder of George Floyd? According to an extensive report by *The New York Times*, "officers need more training to manage their emotions and aggressions as part of de-escalation strategies" (Barker et al., 2021), but these findings are not annual. Where are the police who stopped their fellow officers from doing wrong toward innocent people? How many stood by and watched, wishing they could do something but paralyzed by fear?

The question of who stands for justice can be applied across disciplines, historical events, social movements, and individual lives—big and small, from the #MeToo (Mendes et al., 2018) activists asking for the rights of a woman to be safe in all spaces while exhibiting "her" agency; to the DREAMers (Mahatmya & Gring-Pemble, 2014) asking to be recognized as citizens and humans while generations of Latinx stand on the fringes of citizenship; to the Parkland 17 (Schildkraut et al., 2022), representing multiple children murdered by outliers who could have been discouraged by effective measures of gun control. Yet so many politicians stand by while time after time the fear of sending one's child to school is realized by gun violence, due to a lack of policy regulations. Who will continue to stand by, and who will speak up? Will anyone stand up for you when you are being persecuted, after saying nothing in the face of obvious wrongdoing?

REFERENCES

Barker, K., Baker, M., & Watkins, A. (2021, June 28). In city after city, police mishandled Black Lives Matter protests. *The New York Times*. https://www.nytimes.com/2021/03/20/us/protests-policing-george-floyd.html

Bloomberg Quicktake. (2020, June 15). *Story behind the photo of BLM protesters helping an injured counter-protester* [Video]. YouTube. https://www.youtube.com/watch?v=TW7MHgprAjo

Bugos, S. (2023, January/February). *Congress boosts defense budget beyond Biden's request*. Arms Control Association. https://www.armscontrol.org/act/2023-01/news/congress-boosts-defense-budget-beyond-bidens-request

Lebron, C. J. (2023). *The making of Black Lives Matter: A brief history of an idea* (Updated ed.). Oxford University Press.

Mahatmya, D., & Gring-Pemble, L. (2014). DREAMers and their families: A family impact analysis of the DREAM Act and implications for family well-being. *Journal of Family Studies*, 20(1), 79–87.

Mendes, K., Ringrose, J., & Keller, J. (2018). #MeToo and the promise and pitfalls of challenging rape culture through digital feminist activism. *European Journal of Women's Studies*, 25(2), 236–246.

Multimedia. (2021, January 28). *The impact of raising the minimum wage to $15 by 2025, by congressional district*. Economic Policy Institute. https://www.epi.org/publication/minimum-wage-to-15-by-2025-by-congressional-district/#

Niedzwaidek, N. (2023, March 22). *The minimum wage fight that will define the decade*. Politico. https://www.politico.com/news/2023/03/22/progressives-new-minimum-wage-20-00087966

Schildkraut, J., Cowan, R. G., & Mosher, T. M. (2022). The Parkland mass shooting and the path to intended violence: A case study of missed opportunities and avenues for future prevention. *Homicide Studies*, 28(1), 3–26.

Taylor, K.-Y. (2016). *From #BlackLivesMatter to Black liberation*. Haymarket Books.

U.S. Holocaust Memorial Museum. (2023, April 11). *Martin Niemöller: "First they came for . . ."* https://encyclopedia.ushmm.org/content/en/article/martin-niemoeller-first-they-came-for-the-socialists

CHAPTER 22
Queen

I am queen

Walking through the land of milk and honey

I have been touched

My great Nubian sister queens of Ma'at have been the object of impersonation and adoration throughout antiquity

Like a Congo warrior, strong and fierce, I rule with passion and love so deep I have been forever misunderstood

At war against the attempt to erase my truth

I have been born and reborn as the great warrior Aminatu

Who stood guard over Zaria

Empress Candace of Ethiopia's tactical skills still reign, as a residue

Of my prominence as I drip the life source of my people like tears

Stories of my splendor have compelled kings to kneel when they call the name of Makeda, the great queen of Sheba

Yet I am always focused on the cause

Yaa Asantewaa is my spirit, wielding knives and guns to protect the Asante kingdom, and even in exile I live on today in all that makes me the daughter of Alkebulan

Wrapped in the garb of my beautiful melanized skin,

Adorned by threads knitted and weaved from light to dark, rich mahogany to deep, deep Black of pure oil,

My colors run red to high yellow to Black-blue of the midnight sky—

I am *Beautiful!*

My crown points to the North Star that tells the tale of the birth of a religion,

And my brothers introduced the world to the gifts of frankincense and myrrh

One touch of my fingertip is filled with knowledge beyond comprehension

As I have toiled to build the pyramids that have yet to be deciphered

The sleekness of my limbs tells stories from times of old

From the begotten to the begetting, and all the begetting that's yet to behold—

I am *Bad!*

My footsteps walk the footprints of the Ancestors—

Every finger, every toe, every line at the bottom of my feet is a story of wrong that has been lodged against my skin

My fathers, and their fathers, and their fathers after them have marked my skin with rivers of remembrance—the raping of antiquity—so I labor into history the collective memory of lived experiences

Generation after generation of princes and princesses with caged recollections of their lost glory, knowing intrinsically they are High Priests and Priestesses,

But lost to the journey

The river Nile, bridging life from the tombs of the Ancestors, flows from South to North, nourishing the very bellies of those who enslaved me

We are the undefined Originators

It is written

It is done

My hips the birth of a civilization

A journey of tribulation, my children have seen the lands of Asia, Europe, North and South America, the Great Beyond of Australia, traverse the corners of Antarctica, but are born out of Africa

My progenies have captured the hearts and minds of all who behold them

Like tar

I scar

You cannot take from me without the residue of my essence sticking to you,
And like blood, I will taint and mark you—
My scent penetrating your nose and like DNA I am part of you
Your story cannot be told without telling mine
The spirit of my soul shall forever shame you
Reinventing, co-optation, buying, and selling—
Your trade has no value here
Because who I am is the *Great I Am*
For I created you!

October 28, 2015

SCHOLARLY DISCOURSE

Have you ever read a book or poem, heard a story, or watched a movie that simply moved you—that seemed to fit how you feel and think, and to fill just one metaphysical space within you? That's how this piece felt in its writing and creating.

"Queen" manifested in one of those late-night research hours during my doctoral studies. I was too excited to be on this journey to find sleep when I could, and dumb enough to think I finally knew something after a single year of culturally competent and historically relevant classes, books, and professors. I found myself lost in between the wretched haze of fatigue and inspiration, with the witching hour as muse for the creative and the philosophical combined. This is one of the creative pieces that in its divination was researched, scholarly implementing historical and imaginative ingredients. And if you include 3 a.m. calls to disturb my mentor, who is also a prolific writer, multitasking night owl, and day falcon like me, to ask his thoughts when I wrote, "Like an Amazon warrior, strong and fierce, I rule with passion and love so deep I have been forever misunderstood," you can include the term *collaboration*. It was he, my mentor, the prolific Dr. Molefi Kete Asante, who from miles away I could see lift his head from his own perversive writing to allow the brilliance of his thoughts to unfold and say to me, "Not *Amazon* warrior, *Congo* warrior. The Black Congo warriors of Africa were fierce" (Roberts, 2013). Not to undermine the wonder of the Amazonians (Salmonson, 1991), but this piece is about Africa. That was a moment of *endarkenment* (as described in the Introduction, p. 3), reprimand, and deep learning for me all at the same time. The first few lines sparked an inquiry from all accessible data—social media, historical data, the Egyptian books of the dead, the multiple ancient bounded collectables that have somehow found themselves on my library shelves over my lifelong romance obsession with books, the written and spoken word.

This "Queen" is not the salutation of every *sistah* that a Black woman would walk by in acknowledgement of our shared ancestry as referenced in other pieces. This "Queen" is a historical celebration, lamentation, and war cry, a reclamation of facts that would easily be Whitewashed by hegemonic forces (Jeffries, 2009; Kemet Expert, 2023; Tastes of History, 2022). This queen who walked through the land of milk and honey, objectified and adored, has borne witness to Hottentot Venus (Parkinson, 2016) and the rape (Pokorak, 2006) and villainization of the Black woman's body (Goldfader-Dufty, 2023). From civil rights (McGuire, n.d.) to social media, the Black body of a woman is mesmerizing and scrutinized . . . except when it wants to be claimed by Whiteness. The entire Black world remembers when Beyoncé became Black (Anderson, 2016) in her musical tribute that rocked and affirmed her as the real Black Queen Bee (Steptoe, 2016).

Yaa Asantewaa, Queen Aminatu, Queen Zaria, Empress Candace, Queen Makeda, Sheba, and Nefertiti (Ashby, 2021; Gitonga, 2020; Akinbode, 2021)—all Black women of antiquity tell a story of Black history that has been set about to denigrate the power and relevance of Black womanhood and Black women. These are only some of the impactful, resourceful, and relevant women of their time and today, who are distinct counternarratives (Sekai, 2016, p. 1) to the ongoing attack on Blackness. These are the queens who gave birth to humanity, every culture, every tribe, every ethnicity, every religion, all research, all academic disciplines—"Black people invented everything" (Dass, 2020).

From the Nile to enslavement, this piece exemplifies and is an explication of the combination of artistic imagination and scholarly research. You can also find this poem on Apple Music, YouTube (Di Star, 2020), Spotify, and other music streaming services.

> You cannot take from me without the residue of my essence sticking to you,
> And like blood, I will taint and mark you—
> My scent penetrating your nose and like DNA I am part of you
> Your story cannot be told without telling mine
> The spirit of my soul shall forever shame you
> Reinventing, co-optation, buying, and selling—
> Your trade has no value here
> Because who I am is the *Great I Am*
> For I created you!

REFERENCES

Akinbode, A. (2021, May 17). *Top 13 most powerful African queens: These African queens led men to war, ruled kingdoms and called the shots.* HistoryVille. https://www.thehistoryville.com/african-queens/

Anderson, T. (2016, February 14). "The day Beyoncé turned Black" is the best "SNL" skit ever. *Los Angeles Times.* https://www.latimes.com/entertainment/tv/showtracker/la-et-st-beyonce-turned-black-snl-skit-20160214-story.html

Ashby, S. (2021). Priestess, queen, goddess: The devine feminine in the kingdom of Kush. In J. Hobson (Ed.), *The Routledge companion to Black women's cultural histories* (pp. 23–34). Routledge.

Dass, D. S. (2020). *Black people invented everything.* Supreme Design.

Di Star. (2020, June 26). *Queen* [Video]. YouTube. https://www.youtube.com/watch?v=DACEa8KCdwg

Gitonga, R. (2020, September 16). *Top 10 most powerful African queens you should know about.* Briefly. https://briefly.co.za/78029-top-10-powerful-african-queens-about.html

Goldfader-Dufty, S. (2023, February 6). *Examining cultural misogyny through Megan Thee Stallion and Amber Heard.* The Urban Legend. https://www.urbanlegendnews.org/features/2023/02/06/examining-cultural-misogyny-through-megan-thee-stallion-and-amber-heard/

Jeffries, S. (2009, March 11). Was this Britain's first Black queen? *The Guardian.* https://www.theguardian.com/world/2009/mar/12/race-monarchy

Kemet Expert. (2023, May 9). *"Blackwashing" Cleopatra, you say? A case of moral panic?* https://kemetexpert.com/category/african-queens/

McGuire, D. L. (n.d.). *50 voices for 50 years: Black women, civil rights and the struggle for bodily integrity.* National Civil Rights Museum. https://www.civilrightsmuseum.org/50-voices-for-50-years/posts/black-women-civil-rights-and-the-struggle-for-bodily-integrity

Parkinson, J. (2016, January 7). *The significance of Sarah Baartman.* BBC News. https://www.bbc.com/news/magazine-35240987

Pokorak, J. J. (2006). Rape as a badge of slavery: The legal history of, and remedies for, prosecutorial race-of-victim charging disparities. *Nevada Law Journal, 7*(1), 2. https://scholars.law.unlv.edu/nlj/vol7/iss1/2/

Roberts, M. N. (2013). The king is a woman: Shaping power in Luba royal arts. *African Arts, 46*(3), 68–81.

Salmonson, J. A. (1991). *The encyclopedia of Amazons: Women warriors from antiquity to the modern era.* Open Road Integrated Media.

Sekai, A. (2016). *Afrocentric before Afrocentricity.* Universal Write Publications.

Steptoe, T. (2016, February 29). *Beyoncé, Creoles, and modern Blackness.* University of California Press. https://www.ucpress.edu/blog/20404/beyonce-creoles-and-modern-blackness/

Tastes of History. (2022, September 13). *Dispelling some myths: Cleopatra the "African" queen.* https://www.tastesofhistory.co.uk/post/dispelling-some-myths-cleopatra-the-african-queen

CHAPTER 23
South Africa

Oh, South Africa, please don't cry
Through oppression they hope we slowly die
We give blood, pain, and sweat
But of happiness we are still denied
Still I beg you, South Africa, don't cry
Our parents' tears soak into the ground
Someone's dying every time we turn around
We don't understand, but Lord we pray
Don't let them take our sweet Africa away

We fight and they kill us—
It seems apartheid we cannot end
Children are sacrificed, over backwards our parents bend
They hide our history
The one our ancestors died to defend
Oh, sweet, sweet Africa
Your heart they cannot mend

When will they take notice
Of our suffering and pain?
From killing our people, what will they gain?
A rebellious South Africa to the end we will remain

We are superior
Our oppressors—that's what they say
But they don't know we grow angrier every day
We will abide, but we will not give up unless
They put our beloved South Africa to rest

Oh, South Africa
Be brave and strong
Our people—they cannot hold
Under apartheid for long

April 20, 1991

SCHOLARLY DISCOURSE

> Despite the promises made after World War II to eliminate the commission of atrocities, crimes against humanity persist with horrifying ubiquity. Yet the absence of a consistent definition and uniform interpretation of crimes against humanity has made it difficult to establish the theory underlying such crimes and to prosecute them in particular cases. In the 1990s, several ad hoc international criminal tribunals were established to respond to the commission of atrocity crimes, including crimes against humanity, in specific regions of the world in conflict. (Sadat, 2017, p. 334)

Apartheid began in South Africa in 1948 and eventually ended in 1994 when a democratic government was voted in. It was reminiscent of enslavement with the constant struggle for humanity that seems unattainable for Black and Brown people the globe over. Instead of assessing the facts of this historical event through research, let us address the onslaught of mental health and historical trauma that seems forgotten in conversations around all the ways that war crimes are committed and how Blackness is always omitted as collateral damage, or not worth including in the revisionist history of White supremacists' doctrine. Constantly, Black people are asked to find the answers to their own problems. We are tasked with examining and interrogating why we are always victimized, used, abused, and discarded—always observed as specimens of history without voice or agency. Yet we do, and we do it still, as we must find our own salvation, knowing no one else is coming to our defense. Biko (1978) expresses it clearly:

It is perhaps fitting to start by examining why it is necessary for us to think collectively about a problem we never created. In doing so, I do not wish to concern ourself un-necessarily with the white people of South Africa, but to get the right answers, we must ask the right questions; we have to find out what went wrong—where and when; and we have to find out whether our position is a deliberate creation of God or an artificial fabrication of the truth by power hungry people whose motive is authority, security, wealth and comfort. In other words, the "Black Consciousness" approach would be irrelevant in a colourless and non-exploitative egalitarian society. It is relevant here because we believe that an anomalous situation is a deliberate creation of man. (p. 10)

As Black people, we constantly find ourselves in a series of justifications—justifying our humanity (Goff et al., 2008), justifying why we should be treated fairly, and, even with proof of sharing the world as we know it in the power of intellectual development, justifying and proving our truth. We're in a constant cycle of mental instability, fear, and fight toward not just peace, but the agency to live and be. This is why Black and Brown people are still in a state of substandard existence when it comes to education, welfare, food, and the historical narrative. The cry, amid the pain, against injustice is never-ending, not just in South Africa, Rwanda, and so many countries on the African continent; the same inhuman measures are being transgressed upon other cultures like Ukraine (Aladekomo, 2022) and Palestine (Ben-Naftali & Zamir, 2009). Black people must always make a sacrifice, and historically, that sacrifice is what got Black people to a place of conversation in close proximity to a table we are never welcome to join. During apartheid in South Africa, it took the extraordinary leadership, sacrifice, and love beyond comprehension of Nelson Mandela (Carlin, 2008) to disrupt the process of evil and manifest a historical turning point toward "freedom" as it was discussed. But, even today, there is no real freedom, as every advancement toward Black equity has been met with rebuttal, and police brutality has taken on the cloak of historical racists wearing white cloaks and pointy hats. The mental brutality and ancestral trauma still live vibrantly within the ancestral memory of every Black person. As devastating as it is to constantly live on the edge of defense, we cannot forget what is already fact.

We know that the historical process of colonization was a violent conquest of human beings and the land they stewarded. The violence of European colonization, including the slave trade, constitutes the common history of Africa, Asia, the Middle East, and the American Hemisphere. (Davis, 2016, p. 81)

And while Angela Davis (2016) tells us that "freedom is a constant struggle," we know that the human spirit will never rest until it is, in fact, free. We must continue to seek refuge in the hope of humanity. As Mandela guides us (via Stengel, 2018, p. 135):

> Don't address their brains. Address their hearts.

REFERENCES

Aladekomo, A. (2022, March 22). *Russian aggression against Ukraine, sovereignty and international law.* SSRN. https://papers.ssrn.com/sol3/papers.cfm?abstract_id=4064020

Ben-Naftali, O., & Zamir, N. (2009). Whose "conduct unbecoming"? The shooting of a handcuffed, blindfolded Palestinian demonstrator. *Journal of International Criminal Justice, 7*(1), 155–175. https://doi.org/10.1093/jicj/mqp012

Biko, S. (1978). Black consciousness and the quest for a true humanity. *Ufahamu: A Journal of African Studies, 8*(3), 10–20. http://dx.doi.org/10.5070/F783017354

Carlin, J. (2008). *Playing the enemy: Nelson Mandela and the game that made a nation.* Penguin Books.

Davis, A. Y. (2016). *Freedom is a constant struggle: Ferguson, Palestine, and the foundations of a movement.* Haymarket Books.

Goff, P. A., Eberhardt, J. L., Williams, M. J., & Jackson, M. C. (2008). Not yet human: Implicit knowledge, historical dehumanization, and contemporary consequences. *Journal of Personality and Social Psychology, 94*(2), 292–306. https://doi.org/10.1037/0022-3514.94.2.292

Sadat, L. N. (2017). Crimes against humanity in the modern age [Washington University in St. Louis Legal Studies Research Paper No. 11-11-04]. *American Journal of International Law, 107*(334). https://papers.ssrn.com/sol3/papers.cfm?abstract_id=2013254#

Stengel, R. (2018). *Mandela's way: Lessons for an uncertain age* (1st paperback ed.). Broadway Books.

RESOURCE

Plaxico, L. (1992). *Short takes* [Album]. Muse Records.

CHAPTER 24
Spiritually Grounded

Spirituality to me ventures beyond the mere realm of religion or belief. It's that rare unspoken thing that lets you know that while you cannot see the wind blow, you know it's there because you feel it, and while there is no way to prove love, it's a powerful force to be reckoned with because it can spoil your soul and sink your spirits into rotten meats of disapproval when twisted.

Yet spirituality is the quiet of the eye in the midst of the storm. It's the flowing of deep waters below the crashing wave of a tsunami. And like the Universe housing its great sky and unnamed stars, boasting galaxies beyond our wildest imaginations, it belongs to us all.

It's the gift beyond what religion would have us falter to, saying that faith and belief forces us into a choice of worship denomination, and this is the place where a Christian like me teeters on blasphemy I believe. But what are belief and faith without truly experiencing the freedom that they offer within the choice of free will? How can I dare believe that there is a God who is powerful enough to create the Universe "if you will," with all its great creatures and wonders that are left to be discovered still, and give it limitations? How can I utter faith and believe in such miracles and venture to tear it down into little partial fragments called religion or denomination of the known world, and eliminate that of Buddhism, Judaism, Islam, and who unto us . . . *Sangria* and *Paganism*. What kind of God could be so limited? How can I say I believe in good and not bad? Right but not wrong? The omniscient, omnipotent, and omnipresent power I believe in can shatter man's foolish banter of who is better like thunder and lightning across the great sky where Zeus and Pegasus once reigned, touching without words or hands the infinite wormhole of mystical, subterranean galaxies that house the full spiritual peace of the inner being within us that takes away color, touch, taste, prejudice, and all things that go against the truth of what spirituality is. The freedom of being able to find soulmates and kindred spirits in sisters and brothers who have opened their aura to the light and shine with welcome warmth is what spirituality gives us. It's a choice, one that can see with a third eye the evil beyond mere sight and say, "I understand." It's a gift to be able to open our minds to the things that we cannot see and touch and explain away with science and *know* beyond a doubt that they are real. Like Love!

I have grown to understand and learn what spirituality is, and in finding my spirituality, I am able to be free, like the very roots of a tree that grow into the earth freely and without compromise. I have been able to fall off the cliff that radiates light in the cataclysmic kaleidoscope of colors bearing hues we cannot comprehend and fallen into the arms of friends. And do you think that I refer to me as one individual standing before you? Or am I all the lives and souls and loss and pain and gain and chances to relive and make right that which is demanded by the justice of powers and angels blending forces with the simple and fragile balance of good and evil that makes *us*? Because *I* is *you* and *me* blending into *us*—the commonplace of society that makes up a whole that branches from communities—and *I* is *you* in ways you have not yet grown, because spirituality is a freedom that says it's okay to love that which you don't understand because you have the good sense to know that just because you say it's not real doesn't make it true. Spirituality is the hope that like a child you can grow and be taught by the great gurus of this universe we are humbled to call parents, like Gandhi and Jesus Christ, and not be laden by bloodlines as the pre-proposition of lineage.

Because I am free . . .

Through my spirituality . . .

Inspired by Love and the oneness of *us* that is a small fraction of the coexisting whole!

April 11, 2007

SCHOLARLY DISCOURSE

As a social scientist, scholar practitioner, linguist, and researcher—all the hats I have worn in the almost 20 years since this was written—I am in awe of how much and how little I have changed. This is why I say I was Afrocentric before Afrocentricity (Sekai, 2016). This is the reason I sought the process of "endarkenment" (Sekai, 2016), because while these utterances flowed from my consciousness, I did not then have the language to express or fully explain the "science," the spirit, and the soul behind this, which, for me, remains valid, and which, for those who carry the African spirit, remains valid. Reading and no longer acquiescing myself, without the added intentional rigor of scientific research, to an interrogation has brought me to such endarkening as, "consequently, the uncritical acceptance of the assumptions of Western science by African people is to participate in our own domination and oppression" (Akbar, 1984, p. 395). The same questions uttered in this essay hold true, the same ponderings: *How? How can I not?* And now, through research, resources, and scholars whose frameworks I trust and admire, I may not know the answer, but I am strengthened in my belief about all the questions. "African language and logic are the doorway into the new room of indigenous knowledge as praxis.... [R]estoration or healing must involve the experience of being human itself" (Nobles, 2023, p. 86), because to question is to be whole and being whole is about filling the gaps through our culture and our community. This is why the concept of *being human being* is imperative: "Getting people to forgo what they have been taught in school, convinced of by their racialized parents, and persuaded to believe in by their mosques, churches, temples, and shrines will be a difficult task, but is one that we must seek to accomplish if we are to become a truly human society" (Asante & Dove, 2021, p. 5). By accomplishing this, then maybe we can see with universal eyes, as the verse "Spiritually Grounded" proclaims:

> The omniscient, omnipotent, and omnipresent power I believe in can shatter man's foolish banter of who is better, like thunder and lightning across the great sky where Zeus and Pegasus once reigned, touching without words or hands, the infinite wormhole of mystical, subterranean galaxies that house the full spiritual peace of the inner being within us that takes away color, touch, taste, prejudice, and all things that go against the truth of what spirituality is. The freedom of being able to find soulmates and kindred spirits in sisters and brothers who have opened their aura to the light and shine with welcome warmth is what spirituality gives us. It's a choice, one that can see with a third eye the evil beyond mere sight and say, "I understand." It's a gift to be able to open our minds to the things that we cannot see and touch and explain away with science and *know* beyond a doubt that they are real. Like Love!

I wondered then, and I still wonder, if there is a possibility for this type of connectivity. Religion and belief systems, in so many ways, have been politicized and caused so much bloodshed throughout history in all demographic and geographic contexts. As there have been centuries of no movement toward this altruistic concept, people of African-centered foundations need to find the vital learnings that allow us to be free in the face of shackled minds, capitalistic prisons, and censored voices.

"Knowledge of self is inclusive of information pertaining to one's personal identity, group identity (Pan Africanist), cultural identity and recognition, appropriate and proper values, a national plan/agenda for betterment, and the building of institutions to perpetuate 'self'" (Shockley, 2008, p. 59). Is it possible to unlearn the hate and pain of history so that we might look past the indoctrination to dream? Or do we

> flock to Christian Science Centers, Agape, The Little Churches Along the Way, F.A.M.E., and the local Baptist church seeking ephemeral moments of refute[?] Some of us choose to stay at home and chant Buddhist rhymes, or revel in Deepak Chopra, John Bradshaw, John Cray, or the latest Guru without a moment's contemplation of philosophies which have kept us in good stead historically. Many African Americans have never given a moment's thought as to why we worship the Gods of our oppressors and whether that God who facilitated the slave trade is the same one that will lead us to "the promised land." (Flowers, 2000, p. 11)

Despite the echoes of gloom and the loud sounds of despair around us daily, I am grateful that I have changed a lot, but not simultaneously. I am grateful that I have remained *spiritually grounded*, not in the hope of religion but in the hope of humanity, science, research, and a commitment to dream. Being an Afrocentric woman grounded in the thoughts of African philosophy and political blueprints for the survival of the African spirit, I know I am not alone. I know "I am not the only one seeking answers to the dilemma of being Black in America for I can see anguish in my sisters' eyes and I can smell despair on my brothers' breath" (Flowers, 2000, p. 10), but most of all, I can feel the hope in their smiles, laughter, resilience, and self-determination. Because despite the atrocities that we might face, we are still in pursuit of the freedom of the mind so we can build that which strings our faith and dreams together.

REFERENCES

Akbar, N. (1984). Africentric social sciences for human liberation. *Journal of Black Studies, 14*(4), 395–414.

Asante, M. K., & Dove, N. (2021). *Being human being: Transforming the race discourse.* Universal Write Publications.

Flowers, M. A. (2000). *The door of no return: A spiritual pilgrimage for African Americans in America.* Xlibris Corporation.

Sekai, A. (2016). *Afrocentric before Afrocentricity: A quest towards endarkenment.* Universal Write Publications.

Shockley, K. G. (2008). *The miseducation of Black children.* African American Images.

Nobles, W. (2023). *Skh: From Black psychology to the science of being.* Universal Write Publications.

CHAPTER 25
A Tribute

I am in awe of the courage and strength displayed in the events of 9/11

Humbled by the display of love and compassion

I am amazed that so many could possess the intrinsic value of faith and self

Sacrifice for the good of the masses

And bow to the love that pacified a nation

Bound the hearts of people that time could not erase

I am in awe

I am held breathlessly captive

I am here to spread the word and pass it on as in a childlike verse

The song of the heroes who gave their lives and saved our lives that day

To you who said your country will not stand for death and died—I thank you

To you who said your last goodbyes then tried to stop more pain—I adore you

To you, the pilots and flight attendants

To you, the ordinary workers of the day

To you, the passersby who just happened to be in the way

To you, our protectors—firemen and police

To you who lost loved ones

Spanning across race

Country or creed

To you who were trapped for hours gasping for life—
Knowing and believing that it was just not your time—
To you, who died to save another
I am pained by your loss because there is no other like you
I stand here basking in the beauty of this melting pot of love
A kaleidoscope of internal strength
A strength attributed only to heroes and to our leaders who were left holding the torch,
A thank-you to those who had to keep us focused

This is my song
My melody
My innocent rhyme
Like the child who lost a parent
Forever lost in time
This is my song of closure
My song of letting go
My song to always remember
The pain that you and I will always know
This is my song of serenity
My premature wisdom where innocence is now lost
I am in awe
I am blessed to be here
To pay tribute to you
And I must tell the story
And carry the burden of the memory
Pass on the legacy in a song

October 11, 2002

SCHOLARLY DISCOURSE

We advocate the ancient principles of harmony, order, justice, truth, righteousness, reciprocity, and balance as we introduce humanity as a way around discourses on race and hierarchy—Early African cultures considered becoming human a process like the transformation of a scarab beetle, often referred to as a dung beetle because it lays its egg in a ball of dung that it rolls across the ground. Finally, after metamorphosis from larva to adult, the egg in the ball of dung reaches a new stage. This is why they called the beetle *Khepera*, which means "to become," or transformation. *Khepera* was used as an amulet to reflect transformation, immortality, and protection in Ancient Africa. (Asante & Dove, 2021, p. 15)

Despite the trauma of war, domestic and foreign; despite, genocide, fear, pandemics, loss of life, and the surprises of life, there is one that never gets old. That is the resiliency of the human spirit—the capacity for love, hope, empathy, and real-life superheroes who emerge out of moments when we least expect them.

This is what we saw come out of the carnage of what will become forever known as 9/11. Much like any day that would become a day that would change our lives, a day like no other, 9/11 was unexpected. For those of us who lived in New York City at the time, traversing familiar paths, from Lower Manhattan, to the World Trade Center's famous Twin Towers, to Midtown, to Chinatown, to Wall Street, New York was the place to be in late summer as excitement swelled for the pending holiday season. Then everything changed. People who have visited New York City, or live there, say New Yorkers are disconnected and unfriendly, and you'd better not look someone you don't know in the eyes or you're asking for a fight. The opinions sway, and that is not the discourse of contention. Up for discussion are the miraculous stories of men and women who ran to the aid of others during and after the horrific terrorism of two planes crashing into the World Trade Center, two iconic pillars of New York City (Hatfield, 2008).

Firemen, police, and everyday citizens lost their lives in heroic acts of kindness. People survived because someone helped them to their personal detriment. Limbs were lost to painful memories of trauma, but every single person rose to the occasion in superhero fashion without a second thought (Dwyer & Flynn, 2010). As this piece honors the lives and legacies of those who survived, those who are no longer here, and those who live to keep the memories of those who sacrificed alive, I want to make a point of showing that this is not unique. The spirit of humanity is alive and well, all over the world (Franco, 2017). The *New York Times* did an extraordinary article about everyday heroes like David Capuzzo, a young Brooklynite who saved a man from being run over by a New York City subway train, who stated, "if nobody does anything, he's going to die" (Tran & Victor, 2017). This article noted other such stories. The *Harvard Business Review*, too, chronicled several powerful leaders whom we may all recognize, all of whom found themselves in the middle of a crisis and acted selflessly: "I know that real leaders are not born; the ability to help others triumph over adversity is not written into their genetic code. They are, instead, made. They are forged *in* crisis. Leaders become 'real' when they practice a few key behaviors that gird and inspire people through difficult times" (Koehn, 2020). And on the world stage, the United Nations (2020) found through the global pandemic of the coronavirus multiple unlikely heroes: Nelson Kwaje (South Sudan), Vittorio Foglio (Switzerland), Christian Achaleke (Cameroon), Wevyn Muganda and Suhayl Omar (Kenya), Dana Shubat (Syria), Inés Yábar (Peru), and so many more. "We will get through this crisis. And when we do, I am sure that history will show the world's young people helped to bridge the world from fear to hope and from confusion to understanding" (United Nations, 2020). In this piece, I find a reminder for courage, strength, and extreme faith in the spirit of survival and humanity.

REFERENCES

Asante, M. K., & Dove, N. (2021). *Being human being: Transforming the race discourse.* Universal Write Publications.

Dwyer, J., & Flynn, K. (2010). *102 minutes: The unforgettable story of the fight to survive inside the Twin Towers* (2nd ed.). Times Books.

Franco, Z. E. (2017). Heroism in times of crisis: Understanding leadership during extreme events. In S. T. Allison, G. R. Goethals, & R. M. Kramer (Eds.), *Handbook of heroism and heroic leadership* (pp. 185–202). Routledge/Taylor & Francis Group.

Hatfield, K. L. (2008). Communication research: Falling towers, emerging iconography: A rhetorical analysis of Twin Tower images after 9/11. *Texas Speech Communication Journal, 33*(1), 62.

Koehn, N. (2020, April 3). Real leaders are forged in crisis. *Harvard Business Review.* https://hbr.org/2020/04/real-leaders-are-forged-in-crisis

Tran, M., & Victor, D. (2017, December 18). 19 acts of heroism in 2017. *The New York Times.* https://www.nytimes.com/2017/12/18/world/heroism-altruism-courage-compassion-2017.html

United Nations. (2020, April). *Meet 10 leaders who can inspire you to change the world.* https://www.un.org/youthenvoy/2020/04/meet-10-leaders-who-can-inspire-you-to-change-the-world/

PART II
Poetical Science Discourse Analysis

Discourse is the means of struggle; in some cases this means visual imagery, in some cases, narrative, in some cases graffiti or music or other forms of spontaneous expression that serve in one way or another as propaganda. It is notable that the word *"propaganda"* in Spanish does not carry the negative charge of *"untruth"* that it does in American English. Propaganda is the production of information, simply speaking. Whether it is *"true"* or *"false"* depends on its reception by an audience. (Conant, 2010, p. 57)

THE CONCEPT | THE CRITIQUE | THE METHODOLOGY | THE RESEARCH

There are multiple types of poems—haiku, sonnet, villanelle, ode, elegy, ballad, and so many more—of which my absolute favorite in structured form is the limerick. The poems in this text as you have discovered, however, are very rarely structured; each one simply moves with the rhythm of the emotion that inspired it. Additionally, many of the structured forms of poetry are represented within the poems in this title, sometimes blending, twisting, turning, and reimagining the structures and standards of poetry. Language arts fascinated me as an undergraduate, because not only did I get a chance to read colorful stories, but the pages opened up my eyes to a cataclysmic world, taunting me with a kaleidoscope of colors. I imagine that's what it feels like to be intoxicated, drowning in thoughts and images that can only be felt and experienced. It was a far reach from my initial major of psychology, which I still enjoy, and I endeavor to incorporate library science into my research as a scholar.

Nevertheless, there is a formal Eurocentric structure to poetry that fits neatly into the construct of the English language. From an African-centered framework, we know that is not how the ancestors speak; music, movement, dance, and sound have a tone and tenor that, though perhaps indescribable through the Westernized lens, tell stories, dabble in multiple formations, and combine sensuality and tension to create torrents of emotion. All that mixes with the power of language, in all its flaws and beauty.

Though we are all born into some sort of spoken language, we are aware that

> every experience with language teaches us that communication is frequently less transparent than we would wish. Disappointment at the failure of language to be clear, and at its capacity to mislead and sway us into deception has marked our thinking about language for centuries. Ambiguity, double-meanings, "equivocation" intended and not intended, all manner of "-*speaks*"—"double-speak," "meta-speak"—result from, or exploit, the potential anarchy of language. (Wainwright, 2016, p. 5)

It is this torrential component of words that I love—the possibilities of them, the imperfection of them—and that is how I approach writing, by performing and interrogating the art of poetry. It is not something we can be lukewarm about. We must give our full selves to the art, for the reader to "feel" our words.

REFERENCES

Conant, J. (2010). *A poetics of resistance: The revolutionary public relations of the Zapatista insurgency*. AK Press.

Wainwright, J. (2016). *Poetry: The basics* (3rd ed.). Routledge.

CHAPTER 26
Nea Onnim

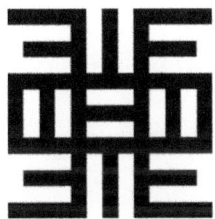

He who does not know; from the proverb, "When he who does not know learns, he gets to know." [*Nea onnim*] is a symbol of knowledge, life-long education, and continued quest for knowledge.

—Adinkra Symbols and Meanings (2024)

The poems in this chapter were also included in the first edition of A^2 (Sekai, 2016). They are left without "discourse," with interrogation technique suggestions, so readers can search for themselves in each piece. There is a synergy in exploring how the imagination can find itself in the very structured world of the academy. How do we begin to write or approach writing scholarly discourses around a creative piece of work? The biggest question may be this: How do we use creative criticism to assess and analyze literary works through a qualitative research lens? In discussing how we can approach scholarly research, regardless of the form it takes, Creswell (2008) tells us to

> present information easily understood by many readers . . . [and] demonstrate how reader interest can be created by reference to the single participant and by posting a question. . . . [O]ne can begin with a literature perspective. . . . [This] demonstrate[s] well how the lead sentence can

be written so that the reader is not taken into a detailed morass of thought, but lowered gently into the topic. (p. 103)

Just keep in mind that everyone's journey to this space will be and look different, but it is only in the journey that words, in whatever way they evolve, come alive.

A new scholar interrogating poetry might ask themselves a few questions to begin to get situated within the art. "A positionality statement makes clear how the identities of the authors relate to the research topic and to the identities of the participants, and how these identities are represented" (Michigan Medicine, 2024). This is an easy way to ease into the topic.

Franco (2011) suggests a few questions to ask upon reading each poem.

1. Paraphrase the poem if you can. You may have a different understanding of the poem than the poet does. This can be very helpful for addressing any problems with clarity.
2. What do you think the poem is attempting to do? Educate the reader, create nostalgia or fear, evoke a mood, etc.? Is the poet effective?
3. What is the occasion that prompted the poem?
4. Who is the speaker? What kind of person is the speaker? Is this clear? Is the tone apparent?
5. How is the poem constructed? What are the units of organization? Is the poet making good use of form?
6. Can you identify the author's theme or themes?
7. Discuss the diction of the poem. Point out words that are particularly well chosen and explain why. Point out words that seem overused or particularly bland. Does the diction help support the theme?
8. Discuss the imagery of the poem. What kinds of imagery are used? Is there any structure to the imagery? Is it inventive? Are there any cliches that need to go?
9. Point out examples of metaphor, simile, personification, or any other literary device and explain their significance and/or appropriateness. Also point out significant examples of sound repetition and explain their function.
10. Point out and explain any examples of paradox, overstatement, understatement, and/or irony. Why are they used? Are they used effectively?

Take the poem "African King" (page 170; see also Di Star, 2020), for instance. Really a Black love poem, it is an ode, a cry, a complaint, a compliment, and a lament all mixed together. There are easy ways for readers to find not just their personal positionality, but also their political positionality. Ethnographic research typically requires the scholar to observe life, immersing themselves in the field in order to gather data. "It is an assemblage of seeing and looking, hearing and listening, handling objects, describing, interviewing, recording, reading, documenting, and working with data" (Ploder & Hamann, 2021, p. 1). A scholar can read the poem "African King" and make a quick comparable data analysis on the date, time period of the piece, and events in society that could have ignited the verse. In social critique, poetry, like movies, reflects life and movements of humanity. With these guidelines, how does a scholar researcher pull a *discourse analysis* from the poem? There is no right or wrong way to interpret this literary piece, but for scholarship to take place, context must be provided. One approach might include assessing legal and legislative cases that have impacted, and can still impact, the sociocultural representation of literary expressions.

For example, in *Loving v. Virginia*, 388 U.S. 1 (1967), a turning point in civil rights history, the U.S. Supreme Court ruled that banning interracial relationships and marriages violated equal protection, due process, and the Fourteenth Amendment. The case involved Mildred Jeter, a Black woman, and Richard Loving, a White man, who, in 1958, were sentenced to a year in prison for marrying each other, as it was a violation of the Virginia Racial Integrity Act of 1924 (Duignan, 2024).

Such topics can be uncomfortable, but the process is not to cause divide, but rather to address the real sociocultural and political occurrences and implications that are still impactful and part of the lived experiences in our humanity. The mission is to *do no harm*, to love Black people deeply enough to understand why things are the way they are, and to not drive the train of anti-Blackness. These topics—especially now, at a time when legislative laws are being overturned, especially knowing the racial history of not just enslavement but the murder of the Black body in interracial relationships, as in the case of *Loving v. Virginia*—can be interrogated. Social scientists can look at "African King" through many different lenses:

1. Racial equity
2. Identity politics
3. Black politics
4. Sociology
5. International relations

6. Interpersonal relationships and communication
7. Media relations
8. Colorism
9. Misogyny
10. Internalized hate and racism

Ask yourself,

> What was/is the mood and cultural impression around interracial relationships? Is it as divided as the political climate in the United States? Why or why not?

> How might an inferiority complex play a role in how relationships are viewed on the global stage? Is the concern only that Black men love Black women or White women love Black men, or is it more important to address the fact that good people are being born into all kinds of bodies despite the color of their skin?

There has been scholarship in which scholars have used poetry to get through the doctoral process, showing the layers and rigor of poetic research. These scholars address the writing of poems not as social science, but as a process to examine and release the individual who must do the research. "We engaged in several strategies, and . . . we focus on how reading and writing poetry has taken us beyond our limits of the traditional and objective knowing of biomedical research, and allowed us to recognize other truths. Poetry has allowed us to conceptualize our research questions and situate and locate ourselves within our research" (Leung & Lapum, 2005). The process of engaging the creative mind, to discuss the challenges of the doctoral process, has worked for many (e.g., Leung & Lapum, 2005), exemplifying, again, how the undertaking of critical analysis of creative works looks and is manifested differently for each scholar. However, it does stretch the imagination of the scholar, making A^2's scholarly discourse unique in its approach, filling gaps and adding to scholarly research.

The literary piece "Any Day Now" (page 174), for example, can be an echo on the lips of everyone and anyone, bearing the mark of reflective humanity. In this case, again, a historical reference can bring a scholar closer to a research discourse. If you are a sociologist, psychologist, criminologist, or communications scholar, do you see your discipline manifested in this piece, and if so, how? Can you pull out any pain or reference points through an interdisciplinary approach?

As another example, in "The Homeless Cry" (page 190) I wanted to address homelessness—especially in the cold, when mothers and children have nowhere to go—and the fact that most people in America are living from paycheck to paycheck. The implication is that most of us are not very far removed from the homeless experience.

Research questions and hypotheses can be as broad or as narrow as you like when addressing the conversation surrounding each poem. Womanism and Black feminist theory can be applied in the interrogation of many of these pieces, while keeping in mind anthropological and political frameworks, sociological paradigms, and a historical lens. There is a global attitude that should be in conversation with all the topics addressed in A^2, but there is also a currency of Blackness and of Whiteness that can be witnessed and experienced, and that may be used and wielded differently by different demographic groups for very different intents. Dive into the characters in each poem and wrestle with the language, the culture, and the identity politics, in addition to considering how technology and media either perpetuate or delineate the challenges expressed therein. But be careful, in considering the overarching view, not to paint with brushstrokes too wide to account for humanity, circumstances, political events, and generalizations.

Poetical Analysis

AFRICAN KING

African King,

When did you forget there's a queen standing by your side?

Silently guiding, uplifting, and cherishing you

We are the ones who bore you,

Watched your pain and struggles to survive like the Black panther of the jungle.

We are the ones who walked barefoot beside you,

Washed your calloused, torn feet with fine oils, then massaged you with the velvety smooth Black skin that curves and shapes our bodies,

Yet, you shun us, oh, African King.

You shun us to prove you can be other than who you are

As you stop touching the kink of our hair

And licking the crack of our backs

Because you've stopped loving what we represent,

Your African Queens,

Daughters,

Sisters,

And mothers.

Yet we were willing to fight for you then,

And now we are willing to die for you

Because as we watch our brothers, fathers, and sons watch the European woman with her straight long hair, glittering jewelry, and deceptive smile,

We hold our bellies and crouch over in pain, and we watch our men become an endangered species.

We put our hands to our ears to stop the chilling sound of laughter ringing like bells in our ears,

Calling us fools,

Mocking us,

African King.

African King,

If we could only see you smile at us once more

And taste the nectar of thick, succulent lips that have defined you,

If you will only engulf us again,

Fill us with your fiery passion

That only we your African Queens can understand

Touch us with those large, veined hands and fingers,

Those hands that can sweep with rage and anger to protect,

Yet touch and give such pleasures,

Gently stroking and yielding,

Raising us to the peak of perfect womanhood and proclaiming us cherished as you caress us into submission.

Move our waist with the rhyme of your women grinding coffee

With the elasticity of a snake and the precision of an arrow,

Melt us into you as we tear at your breast and pour ourselves into your soul, proclaiming you man

African King,

Can't you see we need you?

You leave us no choice but to abandon you.

Your rage has blinded you, and now you are like a wild beast out of control.

We have no role models for our sons.

Who will inherit your throne, oh, King?

Who will reign?

African King.
African King.
African King.

September 22, 1994

Chapter 26: Nea Onnim

Poetical Analysis

ANY DAY NOW

The power of the world of perception
Is duly underestimated
The desire for fame
Fortune
Passion
Excitement
The need for money
To survive
For food
Any given day now I will wake to a better morn
When I won't have to plan and contemplate
The way I must make for myself
When the urge to beg
Make a fool of myself
Allow the abuse in a relationship
For the sake of security
To feel taken care of
Any damn day now
The idea of maybe
The possibility of selling my soul to the devil
Will stop gnawing at my brain
Eating away at the very essence of my moral fiber

It's not just me
I take one look at the world around me
And it beckons me
Calling out my name

Any day now
This dog-eat-dog world will value my laugh in the face of my innocence
Laugh
Laugh
Laugh
At my foolish ambition to believe that my body is the temple of my God
That to look at myself in the mirror as a poor, shattered, empty soul
Was better than a reflection of shame
That to stand in the face of hunger and death
And say no to surrendering my soul for a piece of that delicious golden crisp pie is ego
Not common sense

Any day now
Someone will recognize my plight
Someone will admire my passion
The light from the source that drives my soul will shine through
And my place in this world of contentment
And happiness will be given me as a reward
For the mountains
And the boundaries
And barriers
And tears
And pain
And disappointment weathered

Any day now
This page will turn
This chapter will continue
This character will find the way back to the beginning
And end this book with this hope
That one day
Someday soon
Any day now ...

February 28, 1999

Chapter 26: Nea Onnim

Poetical Analysis

BROWNING

Browning
Slim
Sexy
Browning
How I used to revel in the recognition
At that young, guiltless age back home in Jamaica
Walking through the streets, showing my long legs
Legs my mom used to say resembled that of a scrawny chicken
My tanned brown skin was an asset
The clear reflection of white blood

I used to accept those whistles and calls as a rite of passage
And never thought about their significance

Chapter 26: Nea Onnim

Then I migrated here to the United States
And racism flooded my life
From the hallways in school to the street corners where men still call
"Tender brown chicken," or "Hey, light skin, come here, Browning"
But with the history of Black people in enslavement
With the collective memory of my people
Telling painful tales of rampant rapes
The story conveying the fiction of the skin color complex and the "good hair" syndrome
My innocence is now torn apart with the hard reality of discrimination and hate

Going back home for the first time was hard
Facing the realization that there is a value and elevation that happens because I passed the "brown paper bag test"
Internalized self-hatred
I wished I were as Black as tar
Just so I wouldn't have to feel that I was caught somewhere between loving people of all colors and loving myself
Am I betraying history by walking around with this hue on my body?

Walking down the road on the island of my birth
My mother explained what she could of my ancestry
The textbooks explained what they could of my ancestry
Folklore and bits of historical truth explained what they could of my ancestry
But it didn't help

And the catcalls still came
"Browning, Browning, come here"
After all those years, my people still value the white blood in us over the Black richness like Blue Mountain coffee

June 1991

Chapter 26: Nea Onnim

Poetical Analysis

COFFEE

I am strong, Black, and rich
Some try to dilute me
But if they think that makes me weak
They are more stupid than a bitch

Sometimes I call myself decaf
But that don't alter me in any way
Because the more you drink me
The more you want me—
Getting helplessly dependent every day

Don't open your eyes in wonder
Like you don't know what I mean
Don't even judge and criticize me
'Til you've been where I've been or seen what I've seen

I'm a humble servant trying to help you
In your day-to-day life
Living without me will haunt you—
Withdrawal cutting through your soul like a knife

Chapter 26: Nea Onnim

Please don't be scared, I'm no stranger
You know exactly who I am
I am the support, the rock, and foundation
That keeps you awake, pleasant, and calm

I am all you can depend on
When life has let you down
I will always be there for you
When your alarm clock fails
You know where I can be found

You will come to need, want, and desire me
In a way you can't explain
No need to deceive yourself or deny it
Why give yourself unnecessary pain?

I will make sure you remember
I will be everywhere you turn
My aroma will taunt and tease you
Come on, life is short!
Indulge in what you yearn

You will willingly become my personal slave
Catering to my every will
Even in my absence you will fear me
But I'll be there for you still

I know sometimes I sound scary
But really! I'm not as bad as some say
For when you're cold, weary, and tremble
I will wrap you in me
Warming you like the source of the sun's ray
Sometimes you want to say no

But shit, you can't say no to me
Because by now I own your very soul
Without me, what would you be?

You'll be nervous, anxious, and tired
You'll be edgy because of sleepless nights
You'll have bags under your eyes, very unattractive
Then you'll give in, for you'll realize I'm right

You'll try anything
Candy, liquor, or gum
But the minute you lay your eyes on me
Heaven and hell will know you want some

So go ahead
Taste and try me, my subject
Drink me down to the very last drop
I will pimp you like a cheap whore
Even on your deathbed, you won't want to stop

Do you still think you don't know me
Go ahead, take a closer look
You can call me master, coffee, or
Big daddy hook
For one whiff of me is all it takes
And a whiff is all it took

February 6, 1998

Chapter 26: Nea Onnim

Poetical Analysis

DISCLOSURE

Time
Time
Reeling out of my mind
Out of control, out of sanity
Where do you go when there is no place to go?
When the necessities of life are race and oxygen is sold like platinum?
The circle continued
Round and round
Twirling and twirling
Funneling into an abyss where there is no end
Blackness and Blackness
White light and gray
Blinded by thoughts that have no beginning or ending
Lying in the confusion of my own cyber dirt
The psychological byproducts of my own mind
Wind, wind
And rewind to a place where memories are surreal
Fast-forward to a place where no one exists
Nothing exists
Just me and my insanity
Alone in a universe where there is no shame or conscience

Chapter 26: Nea Onnim

Dead to the world of belief and virtue
Lost in the space of life and death
A death that's ongoing
Never ending
Agonizing
And sweet
I roll around with blind eyes
Bound hands
Handcuffed feet
Slavery is dead
Slavery is past
No, no
It is in our heads
It's alive in the institutionalization of our memories
We are minded by our own insanity
We carry our demons with us
Hell snaps at our heels
Waiting to devour us in our own baptismal bath
Slavery
Baptism
Hell and insanity
This is the way love goes
This is what makes the world go round
This is sugar and spice and all things bittersweet
All wrapped up in a tight, elusive wisdom
A wisdom that we can never attain
Sanity is insane
Time, time, reeling out of control
There is no time
No heaven and earth
We're all someone's joy toy
Hanging in the balance of some giant child's whim
To play

To kill
To destroy
There is no world
We exist in someone's dollhouse with multiple compartments
A perverse version of Ken and Barbie
Insanity

February 20, 2000

Chapter 26: Nea Onnim

Poetical Analysis

THE HOMELESS CRY

Without hope, help, or pity
They dig around in our strewn garbage
Looking for a discarded blanket
Or wasted food to eat

We hear their helpless pleas
And see their ragged, torn dirty clothes
Not a warm shirt on their backs
Or a place to go
They walk around with destitute looks on their faces
In the heartless, freezing cold

Their poverty-stricken bodies
Weak from hunger and pain
Their legs wobbly, knowing there's not much
Further they can go

The homeless cry is still not clearly heard
All the broken hearts and
Shattered dreams
For too long they have suffered
PLEASE, hear the homeless cry . . .

May 1, 1991

Chapter 26: Nea Onnim

Poetical Analysis

I FOUND ME

Today
I looked in the mirror
And saw a woman who wasn't there before
A woman somewhat wiser
Someone who has learned the true value of love and friendship
Someone who has grown to understand
That life is also about loss

I saw a woman who has been knocked down a few times
And found the strength to crawl
A woman who lost faith
And found the spirit to rekindle God
Finding self-love
And learning how to be in love

Chapter 26: Nea Onnim

Today
I looked in the mirror and realized
I am miles away from accomplishing my dreams
Yet I know that I am closer than I have ever been
I saw myself today
Dressed in nakedness
And adorned with feminine curves I denied were ever there
Blessed with Nubian pizzazz
I was stunned to find someone
Who resembled the woman I have always wanted to be
Fashioned by example
A page of pain from lives I have encountered
I nurtured my garden of living
And was blessed to sidestep some muddy waters

Today
I saw a woman glow with pride
Eyes somewhat saddened by life
But filled with hope
I saw a lady graced with luck and silver lined by God's love
I saw a girl
Filled with life and still yearning to live
I found myself today
Glowing
Hair as natural as the day I was born
Skin Black, smooth, and carefree

Today
I saw me smile a calm serenity of surrender
And embrace the mountains I must move
I looked in the mirror today
And finally
For the first time
I saw me

November 8, 2002

Chapter 26: Nea Onnim

Poetical Analysis

I LOOKED INTO THE MOUNTAINS

I looked into the mountains and I saw the spirit of a King
And I heard the drums calling from the hills
Where mortal feet dance
And the flesh rejoices
As the mountains open up and regurgitate the truth
Images of captured souls
Surrendering to the ancient drums
And dance through mortal feet
As the flesh rejoices

I looked into the mountains and saw the spirit of a man
Captured in the essence of a King
Living in the mirror of his ancestors
Basking in the greatness of the Gods
Who were created by one God
Basking in the essence of many Queens
Who were created to emulate one Queen
The man blending his sprit with his ancient soul

A unity that completes the transcendentalism of life
Alpha to Alpha
A blessing
When SOULS mate
A circling cycle of lessons not yet learned
I looked into the mountains and there I saw the mating of our souls
A man with the spirit of an ancestral King
I looked into the mountains
And saw you

November 19, 2005

Chapter 26: Nea Onnim

Poetical Analysis

LOVING THE METAPHOR OF LIFE

I love the metaphor
And I know the pain of disappointment
Remember that as a people we are lost
And even those knowing the truth
Those who remember the good and purity of the days
Get discouraged and afraid
But not everyone is afraid
Some, like you, yearn to go home
Yearn to dance in the sand
Climbing mango trees and making coconut drops in banana leaves
Some of us miss the heart of digging for yams
And growing sorrel in our backyards
But a transition still it is
A transition from then to now
And from now to go back

I have heard your cries
I feel your inner yearning
Appealing to our souls, "our people," to come to you
To come back home and find peace and freedom
Some are still blind, but not all

Call out to those who will listen, and they will tell someone
And someone will tell someone else
And the fire will be ignited into a furnace of hope
I love the metaphor
But let it not just be that
Let it build and simmer until you breathe life into it
That's what I am listening for
The wind
The bending of tree barks
The whistling of whispering leaves
Telling me that all is not lost
And HOPE is still alive

November 15, 2005

Chapter 26: Nea Onnim

Poetical Analysis

MAN AND CHILD

A man and his child,
An unexpected bond formed through love and hardship
You could see them together like clockwork
Holding hands
Laughing
He touches him with a kind of gentleness
Preserved for those who triumph
And showers him with care
New to the life of fatherhood, he seeks
Only to master the art of growing
Instilling in his child all that he knows of commitment and trust
Because mistrust and misunderstanding are a man's enemies

And one day his child will become a man
So for now he sits by his child's bedside
And enjoys the simple pleasure of his sleep
For now he lies awake at night
Sleepless nights
And endless dreams of longing,
Longing to smile again with a brilliance that only the sun possesses
Because Fridays are happy days
It's the day that precedes the two days
He can indulge in his child's desires
When he can feel the quiet anxiety
A skipped heartbeat, as his hands glide slowly
Through the young boy's hair
When he can listen to sighs merging together simultaneously
Because he's breath of his breath
And life of his life,
And one cannot exist without the other
Because they exist together
And live for each other
He's a better man for it
And his child will be a better man for it

Because they are man and child
Missing each other
Coexisting together
Because they are . . .

Man and child

October 21, 1994

Chapter 26: Nea Onnim

Poetical Analysis

OPPRESSION OR EQUAL RIGHTS

Was it all for NOTHING?
All the people who died—
Martin Luther King with nonviolence—he tried—
Malcolm X—for his death, I cried

When will the violence end?
I'm tired of trying to defend
My race. My color. My existence!!!
I am human, or do you question that too?
Racism! When will it be through?

Civil rights, accomplishments we made
We're right back where we began
We have to make a stand
Our strengths and abilities, they won't allow us to grow
We won't let them bring us down; we have to let them know

BLACKS!
You're Black, I'm Black—
You should be proud! I'm proud!
It is a gift and an honor of which we are endowed

Stop the violence, PLEASE!!!
What's going to come of this world?
What about our children, will there be no end?
Will they continue to die and fight for the same rights King and X died to defend?

Dedicated to Rodney King—you are the victim of RACISM!!!

June 13, 1992

Chapter 26: Nea Onnim

Poetical Analysis

REVOLUTION

How a Black man loves a Black woman
Is as much revolution as politics.
How he kisses her,
Touches her soft,
Or moves her in whichever dimension—
How he wants a woman
Or how she wants him—
Is as deep as the whips that cut through our forefathers' skin

It's not just about chains and handcuffs,
Edible draws, and domination.
It's about ridding ourselves of inhibitions that they told us would lead to damnation

So what if we are aggressive men
Shy with the communication factor?
As the descendants of kings and princesses
We never needed to be actors

Our Black men are fierce and powerful in their demeanor
We must learn to embrace and cherish this
Not let it mean we are inferior

Chapter 26: Nea Onnim

All those talking 'bout revolution—
It's not just about standing up, fighting for our rights
Taking up shotguns and bullets, or peaceful starvation fright
It's about not judging, criticizing
Or putting your people down
And definitely not about screaming your head off with that loud obnoxious sound
We cannot just think of protesting
Yelling and screaming until we feel like busting
Because changing our exterior
Will not let them see what's within

Changing who we are won't make them love us
Nobody's gonna hear our cause until we start with us—
Talking and caring is one way to start a revolution
With only political actions and human rights speeches
We'll only keep sounding like a shitload of confusion

Until we learn to love each other
Black man to Black woman,
Until we learn to start with each other,
We will never understand or learn how to carry the pain
The memories that bind and came with us from where the first Africans came from

Babies must learn to crawl before they can walk
They just can't get up and run
They must learn what to hate
Before they can really start having fun

The biggest part of the revolution that Black people must learn to overcome
Is accepting our differences. We must appreciate what our minds can do
And make the best out of the worst circumstances

Even in slavery, our ancestors danced and sang
The masters would laugh and talk and criticize
They would sometimes even join in
They talked of their happy niggers
How content and peaceful they seemed in chains
But we used sharing to heal our souls
And save each other from the bondage that will forever cause us pain

Our spoken and written words must be our revolution—
Reading groups, slams, and classroom education
We have to always remember
That we could not always gather like this
And it really does not matter what the subject is
Or whose backside we are saying we want someone to kiss
We come together to express our souls,
Cry out to anyone who will listen
As we address the tragedies that befall us
And slowly bridge the gap to fill whatever love we're missing

Join together in this celebration
This profound stance of Black love elevation
For whatever mountains it moves, big or small
It is a good start of being a part
Of the greatest revolution to come

June 30, 1999

Poetical Analysis

YOUTH CRIME! NO MORE!

Young brother! I say it's not right
That we constantly have to fight
We have a chance to be free
Youth boy! Don't you agree?
Use the opportunity to learn and understand
That education can give you the upper hand

Stop the separation, think of escalations
So you can help your people unite!
Brothers and sisters, you're the key to our future
Without you we can't win
Brothers and sisters, you're our hope
Without a fair fight, it's a sin

Rap and reggae won't do it
Used jeans and sneakers can't cut it
Killing your brothers ain't cool
That's making us look like fools
What's cool is the intellectual and spiritual learning
Only that will satisfy our yearning

Now, think about it! Can't you see?
You can become anything you want to be
You want power? Look at your skin!
Now aren't you proud?
BLACKNESS is POWER
and POWER is LOUD!!!!!!

October 24, 1992

Chapter 26: Nea Onnim

CONCLUSION

As engagement and conversations ensue with A^2, the intent is that the poems serve as conversation starters, both in and out of the classroom. From poetry cafés to the spoken-word stage, from the K–12 classroom to college desks, there is nothing that does not impact us at every level, in every class, within our multiple identities, and there should be ongoing conversations around all of it, to increase understanding, dispel myths, and destroy the silence and censorship that breed hate and fear. The poetical pieces are intended to stir emotion, while tempering those emotions with strategic, analytic, and practical discussions that grow out of research and studentship. As these poems are meant to be performed, as opposed to just being read, their true value lies in taking off one's personal immediate response and replacing it with story. Provided here are only some of the resources that scholars can use to engage the various aspects of the lived experience. Some great writing prompts may also be found on the *New York Times* Lesson Plans page (www.nytimes.com/section/learning/lesson-plans; see also Gonchar, 2017), which can be used not just for writing but for reading, as well as structural and intellectual engagement, to grapple with all the things that make us a community of humanity.

REFERENCES

Adinkra Symbols and Meanings. (2024). *Nea onnim.* https://www.adinkrasymbols.org/#google_vignette

Creswell, J. W. (2008). *Research design* (3rd ed.). SAGE.

Di Star. (2020, June 26). *African king* [Video]. YouTube. https://www.youtube.com/watch?v=88oEPZacSQQ

Duignan, B. (2024, February 2). *Loving v. Virginia.* Britannica. https://www.britannica.com/event/Loving-v-Virginia

Franco, H. (2011, May 13). *10 questions to ask when critiquing poetry.* HubPages. https://discover.hubpages.com/literature/10-Questions-To-Ask-When-Critiquing-Poetry

Gonchar, M. (2017, March 1). 401 prompts for argumentative writing. *The New York Times.* https://www.nytimes.com/2017/03/01/learning/lesson-plans/401-prompts-for-argumentative-writing.html

Leung, D., & Lapum, J. (2005). A poetical journey: The evolution of a research question. *International Journal of Qualitative Methods, 4*(3), 63–82. https://doi.org/10.1177/160940690500400305

Michigan Medicine. (2024). *Positionality statements in brief.* Center for Disability Health and Wellness. https://disabilityhealth.medicine.umich.edu/positionality-statements-brief

Ploder, A., & Hamann, J. (2021). Practices of ethnographic research: Introduction to the special issue. *Journal of Contemporary Ethnography, 50*(1), 3–10.

Sekai, A. (2016). *Afrocentric before Afrocentricity.* Universal Write Publications.

Afterword

Baba Wade Ifágbemì
Sàngódáre Nobles, PhD

Dr. Ayo Sekai's *A²: A Scholarly Poetical Science Discourse* is revelatory. In this contribution, Dr. Sekai concretizes the special trajectory of African-centered thought and praxis that is distinct from and breaks free of the compartmentalization of Western disciplinary discourse. Until Western hegemonic domination, African knowers and seers shared their knowing and knowledge production, unrestrained by the limitations of boundaries. In effect, we seamlessly blended the arenas of being and knowing. In being whole beings, we mixed forms, functions, and feelings. In this way, our knowers and seers were both spirit driven and spirit defined. It is this motif that cannot be categorized by Western narratives and literary critique. This spiritedness is, in fact, what defines African-centeredness and the African American artist, priest, and scholar as one. For the most part, Black artists, more than the scholars, have been the "spirit keepers" of our cauldron of memory and imagination. The Black artists-scholars-priests have been our unrecognized intellectual warriors and wisdom keepers. The poetics and artistry of Nina Simone ("Mississippi Goddam"), James Baldwin (*The Fire Next Time*), Lorraine Hansberry (*A Raisin in the Sun*), Richard Wright (*Native Son*), Stevie Wonder ("Higher Ground"), Paul Robeson (*Song of Freedom*), James Brown ("Living in America"), Max Roach ("Tears for Johannesburg"), Toni Morrison (*Beloved*), Abbey Lincoln (*We Insist!*), Octavia Butler (*Kindred*), Dizzy Gillespie ("A Night in Tunisia"), Zora Neale Hurston (*Their Eyes Were Watching God*), Marvin Gaye (*What's Going On*), Alice Walker (*The Color Purple*), Cicely Tyson (*Sounder*), Neil deGrasse Tyson (*Origins*), and Maya Angelou (*I Know Why the Caged Bird Sings*) are several examples—absolutely a small representation of the artistry, poetics, and intelligentsia of African American people—of our intellectual warriors and wisdom keepers who support this special African blending of intelligence, art, philosophy, and spirit.

While providing scholarly discourse relative to selected poems, Dr. Sekai does more than provide critique and discussion of poetic contributions.

She, in fact, shatters the wall dividing poetry from scholarship. She does *Skh* (illumination) that reveals the hidden African beingness in our cauldron. In sharing A^2: *A Scholarly Poetical Science Discourse*, Dr. Sekai is a trailblazer and iconic representative of the Maji's ability to "weave wellness" back into our very (be)ing, (be)longing, and (be)coming. As an "after word," Dr. Sekai provides the next generation of artists, scholars, seers, pontiffs, and knowers an African way of knowing and knowledge production.

Baba Wade Ifágbemì Sàngódáre Nobles, PhD
Author, *Skh: From Black Psychology to the Science of Being*
Cofounder and Past President (1994–1995),
Association of Black Psychologists
Chair, ABPsi Global Pan African Initiative
Professor Emeritus, Black Psychology and Africana Studies,
San Francisco State University
Founding Executive Director (retired),
Institute for the Advanced Study of Black Family Life and Culture, Inc.

Index

Achaleke, C., 162
African King, 167–168, 170–172
Afrocentricity, 4–7, 120–121
Afrophobia, 29
All About the Hair, 17–19
  Asians, 22–23
  Black Americans, 22
  chemicals, 20
  hair braiding, 19
  health risk experiments, 22
  reproductive issues, 19
  straightening, 22
  traction alopecia, 21
  workplace, toxic environments, 20
Allen, A., 113
All Woman, 25–27
  abortions, 27, 29
  breaking barriers, 29
  historical events, 27, 28 (figure)
  mortality rates, 27
  pregnancy-related deaths, 27
  reproductive rights, 27
American Dream, 10, 31–33
  capitalism and neoliberalism, 35
  Caribbean citizens, 34
  colonization, 35
  colorblindness, 35
  compassion and empathy, 34
  demographics, 36
  immigrants, 33
  inferiority, Black community, 36
  White intention, 33
Aminatu (Queen), 148
Anderson, C., 7
Ani, M., 79
Any Day Now, 168, 174–176
Apartheid, 152, 153
Asante, M. K., 4, 6, 51, 76, 120, 147

Bakker, P., 127
Bartens, A., 127
Bennett, L., 126
Biden, J., 88, 142
Biko, S., 152–153
Black Codes, 6
Black Consciousness, 153
Black English, 129
Black Lives Matter (BLM), 112, 142–143
Black music, 9
Bogle, P., 99
Bourdieu, P., 9
The Broken Bridge, 37–40
Browning, 178–180

Capuzzo, D., 161
Césaire, A., 34
Chambers, C., 114
Coffee, 182–184
Colonization, 35, 153
Compelled to Be Silent, 43–44
Counternarrative, 47–51
Courting Through the Drums, 53–55
COVID-19 pandemic, 106, 133
Creative works, 2, 168
Creole language, 127–128
CROWN (Creating a Respectful and Open World for Natural Hair) Act, 69
Cullors, P., 112

Davis, A. Y., 154
DiAngelo, R., 7
Diop, C. A., 3
Disclosure, 186–188
Dog Whistle Politics (López), 7
Don't Hate Me, 57–59
Dove, N., 76
Dreads, 68

215

Ebonics, 129
Ego-strengthening, 73
Emotions, 1, 2, 55, 58, 143, 164, 212
Empress Candace (Queen), 148
Endarkenment, 3, 147, 156–157
Enlightenment, 3
Equal Rights Amendment (ERA), 28
Esquivel, K., 119
Eurocentric ideology, 4, 9, 90
European world domination, 78–79, 79 (figure), 82 (figure)
The Evolution of My Child, 61–62
   daughter's perspective, 63
   description, 62–63
   fake news and individualism, 63–64
   Journal of Experimental Psychology: General, 64
   unconditional parental love, 63

Fenon, F., 1, 33, 125
Foglio, V., 162
Follicle Affair, 65–66
   attacks on Black people, 67
   Black hair, 66–67
   civil rights, 68
   CROWN (Creating a Respectful and Open World for Natural Hair) Act, 69
   dreads or *dreadlocks*, 68
   eugenics theories and whitewashing, 66
   Global Africa, 67–68
   hairstyles, 68
   racism, 66
   self-hatred and intercultural persecution, 67
   social movements, 67
Franco, H., 166

Garvey, M., 99
Garza, A., 112
Get Out of My Way, 71–72
   ego-strengthening, 73
   psychological impact, 72
   self-advocacy, 73
   self-esteem, 72
   social media, 73
Glass ceiling, 6–7

Global Intercultural Communication Reader, 6
Global warming, 87, 90, 136
Good Times, 68
Gullah Geechee, 128–129

Halloween, 75–76
   behavioral and personality attributes, 79, 81 (figure)
   culture, 76–77
   European world domination, 78–79, 79 (figure), 82 (figure)
   heartbreak, 76
   intricacies of friendship, 77
   relationships, man/woman, 79
   self-blame, 77, 79
Hegemonic race, 9
Her Name Is, 85–86
   African belief systems, 88–89
   climate change, 87, 88, 90
   fire weather, 87–88
   forests, 86–87
   global warming, 90
   Mother Earth, pain and trauma, 87
   natural healing and medicinal practices, 90
   Paris Agreement, 88
   taboos to conserve trees, Kakamega forest, 89 (table)
The Homeless Cry, 169, 190
Human relationships, 2

I Found Me, 192–194
Imperialism, linguistic, 7–10
It's Been a Long Long Time, 10, 93–98
   American health system, 100
   Black people, 99–101
   comments, Black community, 100
   The Jeffersons, 99
   legacy of hate/racism and homegrown terrorism, 98
   "Redemption Song", 99
It's the Same Thing, 103–105
   American involvement in wars, 107–108, 108 (table)
   COVID-19 pandemic, 106
   Gaza war, 106
   global catastrophes, 106

humanitarians, 107
Letter From Birmingham Jail
  (King), 107
Russia-Ukraine war, 106

The Jeffersons, 68, 99
Jeter, M., 167
*Journal of Experimental Psychology:
  General*, 64

King, M. L., 107
Kwaje, N., 162

Leaders, 161–162
Linguistic imperialism, 7–10
López, I. H., 7
Lorde, A., 112
Loving, R., 167
Loving v. Virginia, 388 U.S. 1
  (1967), 167

Makeda (Queen), 148
Man and Child, 200–202
Mandela, N., 153, 154
Marley, B., 99
Martin, T., 99
Mental health, 132–133
Merriam-Webster, 120
Miles, C. J., 128
Muganda, W., 162
Multiculturalism, 3
My Nubian Sisters, 111–112
  Black and White bodies, 113
  Black feminism, 112
  Black Lives Matter (BLM), 112
  colorism, 114
  feminists, definition, 113
  "one drop" rule, 114
  shades of Blackness, 113

Named, 5, 117–119
  Afrocentricity, principles of, 120–121
  Blackness, 120
  identity development, 119–120
  personal and social identity, 119
Namesake Alone, 123–124
  Caribbean, languages spoken,
    125, 125 (figure)
  colonialism, 127

creole, 127–128
Ebonics, 129
freedom in captivity, 127
Gullah Geechee, 128–129
Jamaican culture and language,
  125–126
"poetry of revolt", 125
Nanny, 99
National Climate Task Force, 90
National Oceanic and Atmospheric
  Administration (NOAA), 87
Nea Onnim, 165–166
  African King, 167–168, 170–172
  Any Day Now, 168, 174–176
  Browning, 178–180
  Coffee, 182–184
  Disclosure, 186–188
  The Homeless Cry, 169, 190
  I Found Me, 192–194
  Man and Child, 200–202
  Oppression or Equal
    Rights, 204
  Revolution, 206–208
  womanism and Black feminist
    theory, 169
  Youth Crime! No More!, 210
Nefertiti (Queen), 148
New York Times Lesson Plans
  page, 212
Niemöller, M., 141
9/11, 161
Nobles, W. W., 5, 33, 54
Novitz, D., 78

Obama, B., 133, 143
Obenga, T., 5
Oblivion, 131–133
Omar, S., 162
Oppression or Equal Rights, 204

Parham, T. A., 54
Paris Agreement, 88
Parkvall, M., 127
A People Dying, 135–137
Phillipson, R., 7
Poem types, 163
Poetry methods, 1
Political climate, 58, 59
Pregnancy-related deaths, 27

Pride and Prejudice, 139–140
　activists, stands for justice, 143–144
　Black Lives Matter movement, 142–143
　wars to social movements, 141

"Queen", 5, 145–148

Reproductive rights, 27
Revolution, 206–208
Rosier, D., 127

Samuels, O., 126
Self-advocacy, 73
Sharpe, S., 99
Sheba (Queen), 148
Shubat, D., 162
Social interactions, human beings, 2
South Africa, 151–152
　apartheid, 152, 153
　Blackness, 152
　Black people, justifications, 153
Spiritually Grounded, 155–156
　African spirit, 157, 158
　Afrocentric woman, 158
　endarkenment process, 156–157
　religion and belief systems, 157
　self knowledge, 158
Storytelling, 55
Structured form of poem, 163–164

Taylor, B., 99
Tometi, O., 112
Traction alopecia, 21
A Tribute, 159–162

Virginia Racial Integrity Act of 1924, 167

Walker, A., 59
Walters, R. W., 5–6
Ware, V., 39
White Fragility (DiAngelo), 7, 39
White Rage (Anderson), 7
The Willie Lynch Letter and The Making of a Slave, 39–40, 114

Yaa Asantewaa (Queen), 148
Yábar, I., 162
Youth Crime! No More!, 210

Zaria (Queen), 148

About the Author

Ayo Sekai, PhD

Dr. Ayo Sekai is an HBCU alumna who earned her PhD in political science from Howard University. Her research specializations in Black politics and international relations frame her as a linguistic imperialist scholar using glottopolitics and raciolinguistic methodologies to interrogate language structures that inform the legacy of oppression and repudiate narratives that impact public policy, politics, and laws, perpetuating systematic racism while emphasizing the impact of international and interimistic policies on marginalized peoples across Global Africa. With 20-plus years' experience in publishing, as founder of Universal Write Publications (UWP), an accomplished industry professional, and a vetted federal public servant, Dr. Sekai collaborates with K–12 districts and higher education scholars in the academy to increase the visibility of Black publications and equity in research. She is a published author, accomplished speaker, and Fulbright Specialist.

SANKOFA

To those who thought but couldn't do

To those who did but weren't recognized

To those who kept standing even as their knees buckled

*To the ancestors whose feet bore holes on paths that
I can now walk with shoes*

*I stand on your shoulders today, so my shoulders can
bear the weight of tomorrow*

—Ayo Sekai, PhD

www.ingramcontent.com/pod-product-compliance
Lightning Source LLC
Chambersburg PA
CBHW062109290426
44110CB00023B/2755